**Karen Kellock On Mental Illness
and the Hero's Path:**

SEASON OF TREASON: Every fairy tale, myth or story of victory starts with overcoming evil or sinning. It is a season, tho' a wretched one--but also a season of favor and remuneration later on: winning. In my season of treason all were against me and I couldn't trust anyone like Job see. The people I met/things I experienced were atrocious but in fearful denial I feigned acceptance.   It was a land without justice nor lines. It was utter nonsensical emptiness and I was terrified.   It was evil powers with a downed hedge, but things always even out in the end. Remember that and it'll all turn around friend.

The Creative Act is a literal structure in nature. It seeds, germinates, and blossoms to full potential. All it takes is a creative discoverer to put it all together.

After the Great Work
Karen Kellock

**A new matrix in psychology
with a general formula**

**All Success is Attraction
All Disease is Obstruction
All Recovery is Elimination**

**Karen Kellock Ph.D.
Ph.D. Psychology UCI
Postdoctoral: UCI Medical**

AFTER THE GREAT WORK

HOLY SEPARATION

SEPARATION IS HOLY
WAKE UP TO WORTH
THE UNIVERSITIES
PROFESSORS FOR OPEN BORDERS
HIGH ANXIETY AND CELL PHONES
LEFTISTS SUPPORT WEAKNESS
JUST KEEP EM OUT
HOLY DISCIPLINE & SUCCESS
TO KNOW MAN STUDY DOG PACKS
THE MEANNESS OF MEMORY
BE UNWAVERING
BATTLEFIELD OF MIND
UNDERDOGISM AND COLLEGE KIDS
JEW HATRED IS TEN TIMES MORE
DON'T LISTEN TO COLLEGE KIDS
ANTISEMITISM ADVANCED BY YOUTH
PROTESTS ARE ANTI-WESTERN
RIGHT LIFE PLAN TO THE END

HOLY SEPARATION

What we learned in WWII is you're either gonna fight evil or be consumed by it. Speak out people!

SEPARATION IS HOLY

Stop acting like he's worth worshipping cuz he's nothing. It was due to trauma you were taken in.

Stop acting like she's a good friend cuz every time you said something triggering, there she went.

Just by ending a limiting relationship you notice a big upsweep in your energy and goals to set.

Change your chaotic thoughts into strategic insights. Make your mind a rod of iron not a blight.

WAKE UP TO WORTH

Before you're empowered to walk away you must wake up to your worth and then it'll be obvious ok.

You gotta love yourself more than him. Once you do you'll see what a joke he is in comparison.

Lastly, you gotta keep your promises to yourself. You said you'd never go back and you did [hell].

If you want to usurp the power of a queen simply put her to sleep then they have their way see.

When he comes to mind, think and vision the word "NO!". Soon he's extinguished/dropped low.

HOLY SEPARATION

When you associate "NO" with him, the subconscious remembers WHY and soon his memory dims.

The more you don't go there the more addictive it becomes to go forward until he's no more.

The more you don't go back the more addicted you are to the relief as fact, a new life whole/intact.

The era when you weren't defending yourself was one when the world crashed in creating hell.

THE UNIVERSITIES

My husband was career military so I see thru that lens, making me different from other women.

They can't just answer the question Yes or No. They gotta give a long professorial ya know.

Who are they kidding? These aren't intellectuals they're flying monkeys for what they. call "professors".

The same campuses who deny conservative speakers are organizing pro-terrorist movements there.

We've allowed colleges to brainwash our children against our values and it's dam dangerous.

Leftists don't know what they're talking about anyway—it doesn't change with a Ph.D. by his name.

PROFESSORS FOR OPEN BORDERS

There are professors for open borders while protected by their tenure and nice quarters.

Need to remove the vulnerable from what's torturing them but I was stuck in a small liberal town.

HOLY SEPARATION

Shame is a human control technology. They call you a "climate denier" and it works perfectly.

HIGH ANXIETY AND CELL PHONES

Those with high anxiety spend more time on cell phones but the calm don't have time to blow.

Wife craves greener pastures tho' her house and cars are paid for and she's satisfied to the core.

They're seduced by utopianism then bashed by reality. The next step is violence and barbarism see.

Has all music collapsed into rap? Everything is globally homogenized, no more diversity just crap.

Keep saying NO to his memory, subconscious knows why, the two will meet and you're free, aye.

Brainwash your kids or someone else will. And part of that is vigorous debate, exposure to it all.

Remember, not a nickel to a liberal. No sending them to colleges teaching utopian barbarism too.

LEFTISTS SUPPORT WEAKNESS

Leftist insanity: if I am a good person I must support the weaker side even tho' I know they lied.

If my enemy is weak and poor I must go along with the world and hate myself as a mean colonizer.

Liberals think filthy. Love a child they accuse you of pedophilia, love pets and they call it bestiality.

He gives me privacy and he pays the bills--what else does a woman need? Believe me, nothing.

JUST KEEP EM OUT

HOLY SEPARATION

Stop bitching about the demons and just learn how to keep em out. The world's full of lushes & louse.

He gives me privacy and he pays the bills what else does a woman need? Nothing, just believe.

You're alone bothering no one then she sucks you in, only to bash you from her moral highground.

Control your mind cuz it's a battle between good and evil and Satan controls you that way girl.

Don't remorse over the past when you lost. It's an anchor to your lower self with a high cost.

HOLY DISCIPLINE & SUCCESS

Talent is important but it's discipline which upgrades life to a whole new level, rid of the devil.

Satan brings you down by instilling bad thoughts about yourself. Actively fight against this or it's hell.

When primitive Satan compels bad things, when evolved he just drops thoughts into the ring.

Three deer were still as if in a salute to me. Uniquely nature gives signs of success & synchronicity.

You're urgently trying to find a solution and then nature gives you a clear sign which is so unusual!

When I feed cows fruits they truly love me. I am filled with feelings of neighborhood conviviality.

Johanesse Verse advances psych theory with examples from mythology and nature: this is mature.

TO KNOW MAN STUDY DOG PACKS

HOLY SEPARATION

To understand human psychology you must study animals in their herds due to biosimilarity.

To understand man study dog packs: jealousy triangles, resource guarding, gang psych.

Let em in and they'll overstay, ask too many personal questions, snoop around & take away.

Most men's minds are controlled by the herd but the superior mind is of God and separate sir.

A profound understanding and command of one's emotions and thoughts: it's a man of God.

Without discipline Satan has a field day misdirecting steps & instilling fear, guilt, embarrassment.

Today be a warrior of mind and control your thoughts, while filling it with info increasing your lot.

You wanna increase what you got. Immature, you're a diamond in the rough/a king you're not.

There were times when mind took me on an evil tangent of depression and embarrassment.

How ineffective and disastrous it is when mind controls you rather than you controlling it, whew.

THE MEANNESS OF MEMORY

Mean old contacts: Say NO to his image, say NO to her face. That's how to control your thoughts ok.

Don't let mind go on a tangent unless it's productive. So far it's just been to beat yourself up.

Saying NO to toxic memories will eventually erase the groove, giving into em reinforces them too.

HOLY SEPARATION

Deep set: When your goals and values are so deeply internalized they become consistent finally.

Stop beating yourself up in memory or eventually it's a massacre against you suddenly: it grows see.

Satan knows we're social creatures so he blocks by instilling thoughts that embarrasses us sir.

BE UNWAVERING

Staying true demands an inner compass which is unwavering and true, not changing with people.

Did it really happen that way, or has Satan repeated the lie so much you only recall it that way?

Lucifer is genius, he knows your weak spots and Achille's heals--if your mind is flabby, not like steel.

Self-control and discipline is a fruit of the spirit. Start today to regard your mind and TAME IT.

My mind went off on a toot all the time. Now it's attention to details in the projects assigned.

I'd get on some resentment as the mind caved into the old argument and the whole day was spent.

My mind was so punishing on me I was attracted to drugs/anything changing what I feel/see.

BATTLEFIELD OF MIND

It's a battlefield of the mind, clear and simple. We must control it or be subject to evil people.

Control the mind, with higher forces you align. Now you show extraordinary achievements, aye.

HOLY SEPARATION

Thrown into psychological bedlam I had to quickly release clutter and develop self-discipline.

Discipline, resilience, a profound sense of duty: Now success comes naturally/you move safely.

Thrust into a path where self-reliance was key I matured quickly/saw the world differently.

Once the seed is planted in fertile ground it becomes the defining point for a leader and a legend.

For me life was a battle of wits, strategy and psychological warfare--and fun days were rare.

The path of aloneness and sweet solitude cultivates this discipline. Stay holy separate my friend.

UNDERDOGISM AND COLLEGE KIDS

It's called "underdogism". Liberals always go for the poorer/weaker despite their blatant sadism.

To pity Hamas is to hate Israel and **FINALLY**: we've come to a turning point seeing our frenemies.

We see the blatant disregard in our friends, the cold ignoring of Oct 7 as an insignificant event.

The university has become a safe space for Jewish hatred--better believe it's being created.

The American system isn't as good as it could be, as one rogue president can destroy it see.

I found myself self-censoring in a limiting relationship, always walking on eggs as I self-restricted.

It's the oppression olympics: who's the most victimized wins while successful are further restricted.

HOLY SEPARATION

The identity politics pyramid is espoused by all the professors: very proudly they lie, fakers.

In this identity politics Jews are treated as evil as they get swept up with "oppressive" white people.

Left hates America so much they're ready to side with any radical ideology that's hostile to us.

The global war on the Jews is now called "islamaphobia". That's the new insane America.

JEW HATRED IS TEN TIMES MORE

They conflate antisemitism/Jew-hate with "anti-Islam on college campuses" of which there is NONE sis.

Knowing you're conservative they pick fights to take the moral high ground. Escape the matrix or drown.

You're silent, knowing how easily triggered she is. She presses on, wanting to start the moral blitz.

It's all pro-Hamas on college campuses. It's the great divide as dumb youth chime with masses.

Those who curse Israel will be cursed. Don't be intimidated by silly minds, truth comes first.

There is little or no persecution of Muslims on college campuses, Biden just wants their votes sis.

DON'T LISTEN TO COLLEGE KIDS

They can't even read or do math, and we're supposed to listen to them? I'm telling you, get new friends.

Drugs, sex and protests. What else do they have? Civics was taken out and America is bashed.

HOLY SEPARATION

They're stupid, and their cruel. It's the abortion generation made callous and ornery too.

The liberal is ensconced in "underdogism". Wrong or right, they side with Hamas despite sadism.

A pause/cease fire benefits Hamas. Even the liberal progressive Hillary Clinton said as much.

ANTISEMITISM ADVANCED BY YOUTH

The international war against Jews is waged by woke, progressive youth [like all dictators use].

We've surrendered to the hard left for decades in our universities and now we see the results see.

They don't know what the hell they're protesting, they're just following suit. It's just a mob too.

They don't listen to anyone but their progressive left friends and they won't hear the facts, amen.

You cannot prepare for a lone wolf attack, you gotta interdict them before they come inside.

We just gotta kill em, that's the only way to stop these guys who are committed to barbarism.

We get peace by killing a buncha bad guys not by empty threats, illogical pauses or unplanned delays.

PROTESTS ARE ANTI-WESTERN

Protests: anti-Westernism. Muslims, anti-Israelis and the left wing, controlled by Marxist communism.

Israel practices to kill as few as possible while Hamas wants to kill the most: keep this central.

HOLY SEPARATION

You can't see what's happening and defend it. The fact that she couldn't condemn it made me quit.

Liberal support for Hamas in America is no surprise, they infiltrated our universities for decades.

NYC found out when you import the world's problems it's not a sanctuary you live in but an asylum.

They hate Israel cuz it's humane, liberal, Western, successful, secure, free & prosperous ok.

Oct 7 wasn't an "invasion" but a pre-civilizational Satanic atrocity and college kids love em.

RIGHT LIFE PLAN TO THE END

Being ever-vigilant adapting to changing circumstances is a mark of the disciplined mind/I have it.

This self-sufficiency is about the freedom that comes from a disciplined, detached mind.

The joy of self-sufficiency is about the exhilarating freedom from a disciplined mastery of self.

Mind control isn't about mental lessons but remaining calm and adaptable in the face of chaos.

Do you have the inner stability to not be swayed by people and events? Few have this my friends.

My problem is the lack of writer's block when I wish and pray to God the constant urge will stop.

Right life plan: Work and create until you die when all systems shut down in twinkling of an eye.

I did this moral manual for you and pray you appreciate the work and suffering going into it too.

It started in 1972, a fifty+ year project. Not quickly done but a strong foundation defining a superior way for the Elect

Never Chase Men

A WOMAN'S VALUE VS WORTH
BROKEN AND CHEAP
QUEENS NEVER CHASE MEN
VALUE DOWN BUT WORTH UP
VULNERABILITY TO A CRUSHED SPIRIT
WALK AWAY GENTLY
A QUEEN IS SIMPLY SOMEONE
LET HER HAVE HIM!
GENIUS TRUSTS INSTINCTS
REPENTANCE VS PEOPLE PROBLEMS
KEEP EYES ON HORIZON
STICKINESS OF NETWORKS
wicked bands
OUR PHYSICALITY
LEFTIST WEIRDNESS
MORAL EQUIVALENCE

Never Chase Men

You don't need a ladder to clean your gutters. To find the higher get rid of obstructions from your lower urges.

Finishing the job means exposing all of it. Now this is gonna hurt but you must to be rid of it.

Seeing things differently you were always alone but soon its popularity with you on the throne.

A WOMAN'S VALUE VS WORTH

Your true worth is seen thru the eyes of God but your "value" declines as you age says the mob.

A woman's "value" may go down with age but her WORTH increases as she becomes a sage.

A woman chasing a man: attracts predators as it shows a sense of lowered value and desperation.

Predators pick up on emotional weakness instantly and take advantage of any woman acting silly.

BROKEN AND CHEAP

Broken consciousness is when you have to beg for what already belongs to you and it is pitiful.

Sex is sacred so if she uses it to snag a man it's witchcraft coming back to bite her then.

Anything that is readily available drops like a rock in value. Don't call a man at his work/be shrewd.

NEVER CHASE MEN

Doesn't matter what it's worth, if readily available to any taker [EASY] she's as valuable as dirt.

QUEENS NEVER CHASE MEN

A real man takes pride in the fact he had to do the hunting, not giving in to a chasing hussy.

A queen never chases a man for the potential for disapproval shatters her self-esteem: bam!

A woman is not built to sustain rejection. This is a possibility every time she chases a man.

The tender sensitive woman is vulnerable to hurts so she continues to develop until a king courts.

A soul tie [which is sexual] can stop your growth or progress since it's possessive and evil.

VALUE DOWN BUT WORTH UP

A woman's value goes down in the eyes of perverted male society but her WORTH goes up see.

A woman's worth is how God sees her: her experience, wisdom and the obstacles overcome too sir.

A woman's value is how the world sees her. It is mean, callous and cruel applied to God's daughter.

Chase a man in desperation and he suddenly marries another without even telling you, the fool.

Every time a man says NO to a would-be queen there's a significant drop in her self-esteem.

VULNERABILITY TO A CRUSHED SPIRIT

A man's spirit sinks with financial failure just as a woman's does with rejection: bummer!

NEVER CHASE MEN

THEREFORE, a woman shalt not chase a man so her self-esteem stays HIGH/she stays elegant.

The potential for rejection is too risky for a woman to step outside of her place, to play the man ok.

Every time a man turns her down her spirit is impacted: crushed. This is not queenly behavior as such.

WALK AWAY GENTLY

A queen spurned for another woman: she quietly wishes them the best & forgets the clown.

Every time she "shoots her shot" and misses she thinks less of herself or becoming the new Mrs.

Hope deferred makes the heart sick: we see ourselves in diminished capacity, blocking all creativity.

Being crushed hardens her heart to the world and makes her more vulnerable like a little girl.

Crushed, she becomes vulnerable to those who should never be in her life and this means more stifle.

The only way I rest in my feminine is protection by a masculine or building boundaries strong.

A QUEEN IS SIMPLY SOMEONE

A queen is simply someone who finally wakes up to truth: she's **ALLOWED** the crushing world in.

She sent out invitations to be crushed! Just stay home and love it while you build yourself up.

When the queen finally wakes up she reviews her chasing history with much disgust.

NEVER CHASE MEN

She chased THAT guy, are you kidding? But due to this process, she was blinded in the pursuing.

Woman's not built for repeated rejection, heartsick, needing affirmation of husband not some hick.

Tho' a woman acquainted with grief it didn't show on her ageless face, never again deceived.

Women chase men now and it's disgusting to any grounded or God-fearing person observing.

His phone blows up at work or play, anytime night or day: she comes before the king constantly.

LET HER HAVE HIM!

To the queens: let her have him. If he gets sucked in he didn't deserve you anyway so forget him.

Protect your rights with man or government or your ability to live life as you want evaporates.

In some marriages the only way she can freely live as she wants is living in separate houses.

The righteous see the trouble that's coming and hide, the wicked go on their way in pride and die.

Mess/trouble: It never occurred to me to just not let those boys in, that's how sheltered I'd been.

Were you playing out an archetype? Why this temporary slip in judgment, were you high?

Her self-esteem is diminished and impacted every time he comes over and rejects her again after.

A woman's overtly sexual attire is masculine not feminine, since it's predatory [to get him].

NEVER CHASE MEN

Overtly sexual attire is NOT feminine. Valued feminine attire is self-respecting: a superior woman.

Sacrifice releases spiritual power then passion plus talent equals giant success as God pours.

GENIUS TRUSTS INSTINCTS

A genius is simply someone who trusts his instincts for they have tact and delicacy as he selects.

You move a mountain by carrying small stones. Daily, persistently doing your work alone.

Narcissist makes you fly only to clip your wings. The contradiction is too much & you can't think.

If he valued you less as you got older he's a cad and a bummer, get rid of him now or go under.

Stop remorsing over bad experiences & glory instead for the lessons learned and coming success.

The contradiction between their public image vs. how they really act creates more friction.

Instead of ingratiating yourself with/bribing your neighbor why not let God bring you favor?

As you get older you'll be amazed at the disrespect and treachery you were blind to when younger.

It's not that he went somewhere else but he didn't love you enough to not be distracted that's all.

REPENTANCE VS PEOPLE PROBLEMS

Before repentance you're in one double bind after another. There is no way out/hell's closer.

NEVER CHASE MEN

Repent and the cobwebs of people problems disappear like dust off a screen. They were so mean!

People problems are one punishment for sin, just as predictable as any natural phenomenon.

If you have a part to play in God's plan, why worry about success if God is your Champion?

KEEP EYES ON HORIZON

To protect yourself from new explosions, stabilize by always keeping your eyes on the horizon.

The devil in the she bully sees Jesus in the lone girl out, hates her guts and targets her constantly.

You don't need to be puffed up with pride or recurrently discouraged: avoid social media then de-age.

Anyone who's great has been thru the silent years when nothing's happening/no one likes em.

Sudden fame for a talent usually means there will be trouble morally if his character is shady.

You do what you can. You work the land, build institutions or revolutionary thought scams.

Yes it was wrong. But the culture itself is wrong: we swim in muddy waters/go along with the throng.

Before your time has come there's no way you can rush it and everything you try will simply fall flat.

You're hidden under God's wings while waiting and you'll be glad when you realize the blocking.

Had you been out there all this time it'd be like a firing squad by the whole mob, so thank you God!

NEVER CHASE MEN

According to them it'd be better if I was a man wanting to be woman than a woman liking her station.

For intelligent people it is hard to find a partner but for the dumber/less choosy the choices are wider.

Californians/the past: they're annoying, don't know anything and always find reasons for hating.

Dating would be hard, dangerous and with potential heartbreak: what a queen can't take.

Anyone from California is pugnacious at first, shooting at shadows and bringing a commie curse.

STICKINESS OF NETWORKS
wicked bands

Friendships can be very sticky: holding you in place. Relocation wipes this old slate clean ok.

I had a sticky network of wicked bands holding me down but my relocation shot em all down.

No plan survives contact with the enemy: Your stance must be engrained--part of your DNA.

The minute I left I had a psychic opening to peace with several problems wiped out immediately.

Relocation is like a magic carpet ride, out and away from the black cloud of history or genocide.

Muse: a person or force which is inspiration for a creative artist. When he marries or dies, it stops.

If you spend that time working on yourself you'll be healthy enough to attract someone else.

For when your time has come, nothing--and I do mean NOTHING--can hold it back, for it's divine.

NEVER CHASE MEN

OUR PHYSICALITY

She was amazed to see her skin problems weren't from smoking but from not getting enough protein.

Complete cell replacement won't happen every 28 days like in your twenties-- but it will eventually.

I was overjoyed to wake up one day to all new skin. No oils needed, total repair happened from within.

90% meat diet with 10% yogurt and fruit: totally new baby soft flawless skin in 100 days too.

Paleo man saw brightly colored fruit on trees, knew it was delicious drink, didn't count carbs I think.

The carnivore diet triggers cell replacement so get ready for a new skin once heavy into it.

Cannabis is a right-brain psychoactive, alcohol is a left-brain depressant which I surely want none of.

Alcohol: wish I could enjoy it but before ya' know it's become a viscious habit, looking forward to it.

Sure they love your cooking but it's available only when it's there not when they demand it or desire.

Before going carnivore it was always about too much fiber. A truck in the gut is how I felt before.

LEFTIST WEIRDNESS

When teaching in the university I came up against some weird philosophy that put me away mentally.

"Intellectuals" posing as children of enlightenment have become pre-civilizational dark age idiots.

NEVER CHASE MEN

Crisis reveals character. We're finally seeing PROOF of degeneration of higher education to the gutter.

"You don't need a degree to work here. We'll train you without the baggage" and we'll all be freer.

How can the universities justify killing babies? Cuz it's an abortion culture & they're all for it see.

Weakness invites aggression. This was proven to me by a gang of youths when I tried pleasing them.

A guy shouldn't get credit for putting out a fire that he started but that's how it is in this era.

This slobbering appeasement to Iran will only incite more sick violence as we saw last weekend.

You may say you're not a dam liberal but it's your stand on these issues which define you.

MORAL EQUIVALENCE

In refusing to call out evil [to remain neutral] more barbarism is triggered against the people.

Just like a wartime president, make it certain that this type of treachery will never again happen.

Hollywood scum takes a break from standing for abortion to siding with terrorists, amen.

A good way to escape moral culpability is to ignore the beginning of the war/the blatant treachery.

It's really easy and they've done it for decades: just ignore atrocities starting the thing anyway.

Only if you ignore what started it can you move into the warm bath of moral equivalence. Ben Shapiro

After the Great Work
Karen Kellock

FAITHFUL MEN
BOUNDARIES ARE LIFE THREATENING
PUT THE PAST IN A BAG
LETTING INFERIORS IN
SEE NO ONE FROM THE PAST
HE HURT YOU ON PURPOSE
HIS CHARM IS SOULLESS AND EMPTY
WHITE PRIVILEGE MESSAGE
INSANE AND IMMORAL PROFESSORS
HIGH PAID FAKES
AVOID BAD RELATIONSHIPS = SUCCESS
FLASHY EMPTY ROBOT
THINK OF THOUGHTS AS BLACK PAINT
IF YOU DIDN'T LEARN FROM PARENTS
SIBLINGS AS FLYING MONKEYS
BEWARE OF PEOPLE!
THERE ARE NONE RIGHTEOUS
SIMPLIFY, ALWAYS
GO BEYOND THESE PEOPLE!
YOU WANTED THEM THERE
AVOIDING PTSD THOUGHT LOOPS
HYPERCARNIVORE
STAY CLOSER WHEN OLDER

After the Great Work
Karen Kellock

FAITHFUL MEN

Don't pin your dreams on people cuz every single one has a tiger inside in the battle of good/evil.

Each destiny is different but won't be fulfilled if one is a people-pleaser. You man up or stay a loser.

People invaded my boundaries cuz I had none. Life was hell as a young naive woman: BEDLAM.

Soon as you lay a boundary they test it. It affects so many plans of users and friends/the unvetted.

They wanna use you up as they wish so they HATE any kind of boundary restricting their abuse.

You may change boundaries with the seasons, when you're ready to move on. That too is ok son.

Who do you think you are putting restrictions on them? For your time, your home, your possessions?

A disloyal man can walk away easily/cheat a lot but a faithful man can not for you are all he got!

We can't be free of someone and angry at them at the same time. Forgiveness is for freedom, aye.

It hurt so much and went on for years, my Season of Treason. It made me tough like a marine son.

AFTER THE GREAT WORK

To be free I must forgive you. If I forgive you I'm finally free of you, hallelujah and goodbye dude.

Great transitions are exhilarating, glorious, and heartbreaking since you're leaving something.

BOUNDARIES ARE LIFE THREATENING

You gotta train people like puppies. These things have to happen or this boundary goes up baby.

Laying boundaries was life-threatening, as immaturity rose up in resistance and surely hated me.

If you were easy before but put the breaks on in fear expect worse as the users react like its war.

Going back in the past is an endless thankless loop. You can't change it so when it pops up, block it.

PUT THE PAST IN A BAG

Put it all in a bag: your origins, the sick system, bad mate-selection, right up until you hit bottom.

Now throw the whole bag out. When bad thoughts pop up see the whole bag and throw it out again.

Like as if you were in a war: "I'm gonna throw out WWII and keep the rest". Throw the bag out/soar.

"We will kill anyone who brings disunity with the facts." Stalin during the Soviet Russian reign of terror.

You have to cut off those party members to keep it free of disease and infection. Joseph Stalin

You fell due to an undertow that preceded you. But then you blamed yourself as they did too.

AFTER THE GREAT WORK

What I learned was: people will take advantage of you if you let em. It's up to YOU so forget THEM.

LETTING INFERIORS IN

You were half mad so you wanted inferiors around but then they dragged you WAY further down.

Carnivore was an entirely new trip for me and I had to adapt to a new consciousness also see.

It was a new energy. It seemed strange, like it wasn't me. It wasn't, it's in the proper FOOD see.

I slept when I needed it but basically existed on cat naps. I couldn't lie in bed, I was up and at it.

My life's work is done: [22] 300-page textbooks. The Creative Act is complete and it's getting looks.

Skin problems from low protein: It's the only malady with such a simple solution: just eat meat!

All's resolved with the folks too: got the hell outa Dodge/relocated to a happy home with view.

SEE NO ONE FROM THE PAST

I see NO ONE from the old life. A complete and total shift into a new gear without relapse/fear.

The violence, misery and humiliation I experienced as a child repeated itself until I left: NEW STYLE.

It was like a template in the brain that kept me down, humiliated and drained: no boundaries ok.

Dictators without fathers had no limits imposed so when they killed it was millions, young/old.

AFTER THE GREAT WORK

With high boundaries every day/minute is my own. I write the script, not reacting to dictators around.

The narc makes you suffer for irritating him to maintain control for various evil reasons, who knows.

HE HURT YOU ON PURPOSE

He hurts you to make himself feel stronger, and this will ALWAYS, ALWAYS be the case my daughter.

My biggest hurdle was accepting he hurt me on purpose, with full intentionality. It's Satan see.

The answer is he does not love you [or he would not hurt you] for he only loves himself Sue.

It's hard to understand when you're normal and don't operate this way. But you must get hep ok?

Love what you have today cuz it could be removed suddenly--that's what I've learned from history.

You were a slave at bottom of the social ladder but rose up to powerful influence on great matters.

Most churches today are teaching self-help man-centered wisdom that is not Christian.

HIS CHARM IS SOULLESS AND EMPTY

He's soulless, empty. His personality is a composite of parts he borrows from others: a phony.

Your respiratory problems from being bullied and censored: you couldn't talk/became a cougher.

You've been eclipsed by other personalities. Let all energy come within you now, please.

AFTER THE GREAT WORK

They moved and didn't even let you know. You thought you were friends but people come and go.

He must either tear you down or not give you a step up because he wants you equal or below him.

He praisebombed you then ignored you. You lost your identity thusly and your self esteem too.

Experiencing disrespect assassinates your identity. It quickly dims you and kills your personality.

See all bad people experiences as your necessary inoculation to enable new freedom.

S. Dakota would've meant extreme climate adaptations. We'll stick to mild climate and EXPAND.

What taught us better than anything else? Our losses of dignity and public humiliations I guess.

Living in a mild climate frees up incredible time. I'm not going to S. Dakota tho' the beauty's sublime.

Stating biblical truth gets you fired with your life uprooted and ridiculed/never again admired.

WHITE PRIVILEGE MESSAGE

If you're white you're privileged. If you don't recognize that you're a piece of shit/dim witted.

If they say you lack credibility that makes you a liar and soon you can't count on anything anymore.

Sticking your neck out is what builds civilization. There's always a current blocking it son.

When God tells you to do something you gotta do it. Tho' the herd will call you crazy, just intuit.

AFTER THE GREAT WORK

Narcissism is a shame-based fear of being ordinary, the only way to escape this plight every day.

INSANE AND IMMORAL PROFESSORS

America needs a moral revolution and the first stage is purgation of trash in the university platform.

The professor doesn't know what he's talking about and talks in endless circles/what a nut.

I have never heard such useless circuitous ranting about nothing by a "professor" phony.

He sounded insane, pulling in 1/4 million a year for his inscrutable [and often immoral] rantings.

The professor's view of things is for "freedom" but it's so callous in its emptiness/no restrictions.

Looking back they all seemed that way: perverse, callous--phony virtue/inner hate.

I couldn't stand the professor's arrogance, as if he was superior despite his low/silly/puerile rants.

They stop learning/searching as if they know it all now. They are closed-minded narcissists y'all.

HIGH PAID FAKES

The professor made $250,000 a year trashing all decent tried and true traditions as a seer.

Not only did professor pervert the morals of students, he promoted profs having sex with such!

You gotta be so sure of yourself no one intimidates you intellectually ever again. BOLD freedom.

AFTER THE GREAT WORK

Saying you'll do something then not doing it is lying. Promises broken are signs of lowness, aye.

Fair weather climates free you up so much. The creativity and found time for the HUNCH.

Extreme climate adaptations are survival related and draining. It's not for me esp. at this age see.

In fair climates every day's perfect if it's up to you. In extreme climates it's up to the weather dude.

People want SIMPLER lives with age. They go to fair places: complex adaptations are a cage.

Every day's perfect if there are no surprises. I want total control and fair weather allows this guys.

Success doesn't take work so much as discipline, and this self-control's a fruit of the spirit son.

Some things only take a few minutes a day, but to do them comes from self-discipline ok.

What you pray for you may have to sacrifice for. The less you do that/go there, success is sure.

AVOID BAD RELATIONSHIPS = SUCCESS

The more you avoid bad relationship the closer you get to your goals as an individual rising up.

It's too easy to lurk online. The less you go there, the closer you are to destiny and God my dear.

One takes the good life in fair weather for granted 'til he moves to an extreme area not well planned.

The more you avoid him and don't go there the higher your self-esteem rises and is rescued dear.

AFTER THE GREAT WORK

It's too dam easy to lurk so if your problem's online, use this to build self-discipline/esteem, aye!

Whoever you watch online takes over your mind and can ruin your day as their demons align.

See it for what it is: your refusal to be infected ever again by someone who is NOT YOUR FRIEND.

How many days were ruined by other people? Count the ways for all life is a battle of good vs. evil.

Refuse to spend one more minute whimpering over petty people and they're all petty if hurtful.

When things go smoothly natives get restless and stir up trouble. I'm done with this aren't you girl.

My home is filled with windows. I wash 5 a day: with proper planning it takes five minutes or so.

Going there is like purposely soiling yourself. Why would you do that? Get a grip, be well.

FLASHY EMPTY ROBOT

He's a flashy smiling empty robot who when you go there splatters you with thick black muck.

Think of the sadistic empty narcissist like that, just waiting for you to drop your guard and go back.

A pit viper ready to strike whenever you think this time he'll be nice. Think of him as your VICE.

Just when you're happy he'll make you the most miserable you've ever been, that's his sin.

He's a bloody pit viper in your cage whenever you think of him ok: go no-contact in your MIND I say.

AFTER THE GREAT WORK

Bad relationship is an obstacle Satan puts in your path when rising up to your own glory Lass.

Decide to never be hurt by this person again. Put yourself in God's hands, your One Friend.

See bad relationship as your TEST your must pass to get to success. Readers, it's that serious.

Get outa this boiling cauldron of a bad relationship which keeps you sad, stewing, feeling down.

Just when you heal he comes around again. That's the predictable way it is but girl: DON'T GIVE IN.

Germany has 700 alien gang rapes a year. Why German men put up with this is perplexing/weird.

A gang rape could last for days as new men circulate thru. There's nothing more terrifying I say.

Even a petty crook is condemned to marginality and living an unremarkable life. Repent to live.

THINK OF THOUGHTS AS BLACK PAINT

Every time you think of him it's a can of black paint on your head so control your thoughts instead.

I felt owned, possessed, used, disregarded and stepped on before being totally discarded.

I felt owned, possessed, used, stepped on and disregarded before being totally discarded.

I know what cruelty is like, I've seen many women screw their husbands legally in divorce, yikes.

Simplicity doubles your greatness. Don't get tangential in talk and stay on the beam: you got this.

AFTER THE GREAT WORK

A gang rape could last for days as new men circulate thru. There's nothing more terrifying Sue.

Dependency on people is a giant delusion. For they come and go but God's always here son.

Liberals act like a curb on perversions is an assault on their existence and aren't we sick of this?

IF YOU DIDN'T LEARN FROM PARENTS

If you don't learn it from parents then I hate to think of what you're gonna go thru instead kids.

The world's ways of teaching are hard, often from anonymous strangers like Nazi guards.

It's no matter if you're born rich if mom was a bitch and never set limits on you, not even an inch.

If mom was a drunk you got away with a lot but in the world you're about to be hated and fought.

If parents are drunk/unaware you're stealing their liquor you may think life is easier, until later.

Cuz the world won't take this shit, I found that out quick. You came from a home riddled with sick.

It's a rough world and if parents don't prepare you—with good graces & manners--you're screwed.

Children of alcoholics will be loners or surrounded by other losers until they learn the ropes sir.

SIBLINGS AS FLYING MONKEYS

Are your sisters your narcissistic mother's flying monkeys? This gang up will be torture honey.

AFTER THE GREAT WORK

You have brilliant educated babies who have no idea how to act or what to think, just rinky dink.

True creativity of a genius is global and real, unfiltered by local politics or what the feminists feel.

Build courage and confidence by never going back to the habit/nuisance and soon it's success.

Maybe I've learned way too much history but I know what people are like and I no-like, yikes.

You catch his fancy but so do many others. Don't get caught up or pay price of a stable of losers.

You're happy in the here and now but sad looking back. Doesn't that give a clue what to do in fact?

Up to now you thought he was "the link" to all your dreams but now we see he's just a fink it seems.

BEWARE OF PEOPLE!

Beware of people, they cause destruction. Left to your own everything's in order for success son.

God puts ONE up as He puts ANOTHER down. Success isn't from east or west but from above.

Either he eclipses your life or you wipe him out, it's your choice. A trauma bond will kill you Lass.

Self-rejection leads to people-pleasing. When we don't accept ourselves we kiss up/look up to others.

The world is full of devils feeding off the insecure who desperately wanna be loved and revered.

People who love themselves as God loves them won't up with controllers: they set boundaries sir.

AFTER THE GREAT WORK

The worse loneliness is to not be comfortable with yourself then seeking one to make you well.

A wisened older woman knows no one cares so she only gives out—what else can you do dear?

THERE ARE NONE RIGHTEOUS

There is none righteous, not even one. There is none who does good, not even one. Rom 3: 10

What a modern church has dispelled is the seriousness of sin, the reality of God's wrath and hell.

Ah, the feeling of going beyond a problem, as a brand new vista opens and you're in the mon.

Stop reviewing the past when ridiculed by idiots, yikes. They're homeless but you're at the heights.

It's when you're in safety that you have PTSD cuz now you have time to re-experience hell see.

You're so unusual they believed he worst. That's the Dunning-Kruger effect, the dumb curse.

SIMPLIFY, ALWAYS

SIMPLIFY, always. Watch the uphill movie with music and forget the rest then reassemble sis.

Cut down on complexity to save your life see. Then the RIGHT thought pops up from a calm sea.

Simplify the specter presented to the soul. In your environment, past times, associates and all.

It'll happen SUDDENLY because mass attractions are immediate. Prepare for fame/think of it.

AFTER THE GREAT WORK

The horrors of my history all come down to me giving into people invading me without announcin'.

When I lost my solitude I lost my sovereignty cuz to adapt to the dumb is hellish treachery.

One PTSD symptom is horror at the past. You're waking from anosognosia, denying the whole mess.

It doesn't matter whether "they" know it. God knows it, the universe sees it and so you rest on that.

To be cast in a most unfavorable light, yet you're not: you're a nice person, reliable, a good guy.

GO BEYOND THESE PEOPLE!

Go beyond these people, let em be past relics perished. Go on with lessons learned, encouraged.

Go beyond these people, mere archetypes in the night. Learn lessons, end all grudges, live right.

The older I get the more careful I am cuz I know what can happen. Suddenly too if not awoken.

You were right, they were in the wrong. But because they're a majority you took the blame hon'.

Pneumaticity: make a space so a new situation can come in ok. Reject what's not right for high pay.

Expect people to be upset that your boundary exists. There's no respect sis, all relatives it affects.

PTSD from past trauma lessens with the realization WE brought it on, even sending out invitations!

YOU WANTED THEM THERE

AFTER THE GREAT WORK

You **WANTED** those creeps in your house since you were weighed down with sins/debauched.

Due to the low self-esteem of all addicts, you needed the approval of those users and abusers.

Addicts fall to lower companions and half my life ago it happened teaching me my greatest lessons.

It's all so inferior I just wanna be alone. I always wanna get away/go home for solitude is my throne.

All problems came from involvement with other people. Alone I was on top/creative/free of evil.

The most sadistic camp guards were women. Given absolute authority demons came out: vermin.

AVOIDING PTSD THOUGHT LOOPS

Having acknowledged that you brought it all on, now you can be what God wants, i.e. **HAPPY** son.

Worse development: Living without a fence was like being invaded by armies of demons hell-bent.

Much PTSD repetition is from being angry at yourself for being such a dunce in the said event.

Why go back? It's a thought loop that's never resolved since you made a mistake--it happens dove.

You made a mistake but **LEARNED** from it ok, so going back is wasteful repetition trashing the day.

Sin brings terrible anxiety and separation from God, destiny, selfhood and others in the vicinity.

Keep reminding yourself that God wants you to enjoy this day, to be happy not remorseful/afraid.

AFTER THE GREAT WORK

I was put thru a furnace and meat grinder to make gold: transform. Then I was young not old, adored.

It's two gang rapes a day in the invaded west ok? But if we complain we're racists so there it lays.

HYPERCARNIVORE

The protein builds, the fruit cleans. Hyper-carnivore diet using fruit is perfect with 75% meat.

As body composition changes from fat to muscle you may weigh more tho' you're small now.

STAY CLOSER WHEN OLDER

As you get older, stay closer. That means your HOME where you walk tall undistracted, it's cozier.

Forget it. Those people don't exist anymore, it's water under the bridge, now open to the future.

Our completed works are a kernel which attracts pollination. While waiting continue restin'.

As for the books, I did what God told me to do and I'm living in my reward anyway, totally renewed.

When the Hedge is Down

PEOPLE COME AND GO: LET EM
CONSTANT DEFLATION
WHEN IN PRECARIOUS POSITIONS
BREATHROUGH ANXIETY: THE WAIT
AVOID PAST THOUGHT LOOPS
WHEN GOD DECIDES IT'S TIME
ANTI-SOCIAL IS GODLY
THE FALSE CHURCH LOVES SOCIALS
WHEN PEOPLE LEAVE YOUR LIFE
THE HAIR-PULLING WAIT
REJECTION IS GOD'S REDIRECTION
REJECTION FOR EXISTENCE
STOP SEARCHING PAST ACTORS
SHAKE OFF HIS DUST!
OLD COMFORTS = NEW CONFLICTS
WATCH SCENIC DRIVE VIDEOS
BODY RECOMPOSITION

When the Hedge is Down

PEOPLE COME AND GO: LET EM

People come and go but if you're in sin out come officious demons and little gremlins.

They don't know what they do but given the go-to Satan takes over on hitting the target, you.

What's happened is the hedge is down and you've lost all boundaries. Evil flows in without apology.

Don't have PTSD over specific actors in this process. See it as universal: what sin creates in us.

I was invaded by a gang cuz sin had already torn my protection down. See this sequence now.

CONSTANT DEFLATION

Adapting to others was hell on earth for me. I always saw a better way of doing things see.

Narcissistic abuse is constant deflation and disappointment--how's the body taking it?

His constant desire for approval from any and all avenues is what seals the deal against this heel.

Just as he professes love he seeks approval from some young chick, a pattern that's permanent.

WHEN THE HEDGE IS DOWN

Constant disappointments/deferred hopes wrecked the body because it's not under your control.

Up and down, up and down: a superior female would never be on the begging end with this clown.

Especially being so sensitive, it's been a rough ride: A humiliating defeat, but let me be your guide.

Now, finally, your days are happy cuz YOU'RE in control, not some dangerous and narcissistic soul.

WHEN IN PRECARIOUS POSITIONS

I was in such a precarious position--the future was uncertain--but God was my Guardian.

I finished my work and am living in my reward. It's about enjoyment, home, the pets I adore.

Don't give in to a thought loop. You made a mistake so going back will never relieve, just forgive you.

You just go back to correct your mistake but since that's impossible it's wasted energy ok.

Realizing our problems are universal takes the sting out. Have gratitude: in comparison you lucked out.

BREATHROUGH ANXIETY: THE WAIT

Seasons change, so let them. PTSD freezes us in old bedlam so why not forgive and go on ahead.

You must be sure of breakthrough, a promise of God. Knowing that, just prepare to be awed.

Doubt blocks God so stay steadfast on your wait, in complete faith: that's maturity in thought.

WHEN THE HEDGE IS DOWN

Allow this process [the wait] to happen so when it hits you're completely mature and crackin'.

Everyone seems to be blessed but you. You question God, the project, whether He even approves.

The WAIT is part of the Creative Act. You complete your work, plant a seed and WAIT: it's a test in fact.

Having faith in the Creative Act implies faith in a Creator putting it together and success as fact.

So WAIT. It WILL happen, you're continually moving towards it. The day and time, only God knows it.

AVOID PAST THOUGHT LOOPS

Don't focus on past humiliations but on how superior is your present position: it's a ladder son.

Once you're sure of God's promised breakthrough you can relax and just prepare, mind renewed.

Stop recalling enemies for they're now gone, dead or in jail. Keep comparing you to those who failed.

See the evolution of life as goodness always wins out over the demon strife. Suffer then live right.

Of course you experienced demonic strife, that's what made you eventually choose good for life.

Don't go back, you can never fix it but take pride in overcoming it and learning lessons from it.

WHEN GOD DECIDES IT'S TIME

When God decides it's time nothing can stand in the way. At obstructors He sneers with hilarity.

WHEN THE HEDGE IS DOWN

WAIT to be taken on a red carpet with style cuz your Father in heaven planned every detail of it all.

That's right: the LINK to success is planned just as the Creative Act is, so don't worry about this.

If you are a creative discoverer you've been abused from going against the grain with anything new.

ANTI-SOCIAL IS GODLY

I know what it's like misjudged by inferiors in control, who couldn't possibly understand at all.

That cute guy was just an illusion in your trauma stung mind. And he never thought of you again, aye.

I always felt imposed upon, invaded and tyrannized. I was born Americana independent guys.

Worse were conformist churches, acting like personal reclusion was an affront to God [the witches!]

THE FALSE CHURCH LOVES SOCIALS

The false church would see the anti-social as wicked since the traditions of men are socially driven.

After relocating there's still much adapting as it's now safe to feel/express the PTSD in full flowering.

It took me a few years to fully masticate, digest and eliminate the hell I'd been through to date.

Altho' it's true I brought in on, it was still hell as I was put thru a meat grinder learning my lessons.

You may have to learn boundaries the hard way. To be robbed by Jezebel or discarded by narc boy.

WHEN THE HEDGE IS DOWN

Nip it in the bud. If they can't get into your house they can't argue and destroy your mind or bod.

Remember this in the wait: that we serve a God who makes a way where there seems to BE no way.

Enduring the wait with patience is God's will and ensures what He has promised us still.

WHEN PEOPLE LEAVE YOUR LIFE

Your future is never connected to those who left but to those who stayed: remember that ok.

God removes them if they've become a crutch or when your vision is being cleared for that hunch.

God will remove one when he has someone far better suited for you or when they have a job to do.

When one leaves your life shout for joy for it means something's far better for you to thrive/enjoy.

God couldn't send His spirit til Jesus left us. He's always preparing something better sis.

When you're left all alone be the happiest. It's the surest sign something huge is about to burst.

THE HAIR-PULLING WAIT

The Tsunami is totally quiet before it bursts cataclysmic. See this silence that way quick.

Change your view: Disdain him for not putting you first or choosing you. THIS is self-esteem Sue.

You're alone cuz those people don't fit. They were just scaffolding while you were in development.

WHEN THE HEDGE IS DOWN

Many panic with this solo stage, grabbing at straws or trying anything to get famous or be the rage.

Unlike the impatient losers, you GLORY in this era of solitude and confident waiting to be winner.

For when your time comes NOTHING will hold you back and the new wonderful life has begun.

God puts His voice in you and like in a trance you've just given a world-shaking historical interview.

This tedious, hair-pulling wait is both the test of your maturity and your filling out permanently.

Let perseverance do it's perfect work. Don't cut it off or use your self-sufficiency for premature birth.

REJECTION IS GOD'S REDIRECTION

If He removes people He will bring better. Like a deeper dependence on Him, our Champion/Arbiter.

He eliminates people to clear your vision to SEE what He has for you. Time wasters blocked this Sue.

They cannot fulfill your purpose so LET THEM GO. Let it all be and just look forward to your jubilee.

They sucked the air outa the room, they rained on your parade and prognosticated your doom.

Every time you "went there" physically or virtually you got hurt. Take note of this and avoid/revert.

REJECTION FOR EXISTENCE

People's rejection can be God's direction and protection. Looking back, it saved your life son.

WHEN THE HEDGE IS DOWN

When God removes the narcissist thank Him heartily because now, finally, you can begin to exist.

You'd better hope you're alone or it means your time has not come/you resume your wait at home.

Celebrate being ALONE cuz it means your time has COME and now you relax and get a glow.

You'd better hope you're alone or it means your time has not come/you resume your wait at home.

I don't like you as a star, I liked you much better before. Now it's all about you and what a bummer.

STOP SEARCHING PAST ACTORS
It's all the archetypes

Stop looking up past actors. They were mere archetypes not personal factors/who cares.

It doesn't matter what he's thinking/doing. It's the interaction between you guys & it's gone, nothing.

It doesn't take much for normal people to become the most feared monsters. Prison Camp survivor

If you don't go there he can't hurt you. Curb masochistic curiosities and stay cute.

Joseph would never go to Egypt if his brothers hadn't sold him. Rejection is God's redirection.

God repositions you to a place you'd never go UNLESS you got rejected: His plan, perfectly executed.

SHAKE OFF HIS DUST!

You're to shake off the dust and go to the next city but how can you till rejected from here finally?

WHEN THE HEDGE IS DOWN

You'd never leave any other way. You're too comfortable, someone has to sack you ok.

God will never reject you but people will reject you and God will use that. Remember that and relax.

You go when the place of provision in a previous season has become a place of pain in this season.

Just because it was the good ol' days doesn't mean it anymore, you have to leave or be tortured.

God will stir up the nest when it's your time to fly. He must kick you out due to misplaced loyalty.

It used to be good but now it's too toxic to stay. You must move with the seasons for divine pay.

Your world is the sky but you're living in the nest. You're an eagle but living like a chicken I guess.

OLD COMFORTS = NEW CONFLICTS

What used to bring you comfort now brings conflict. You're not the center of God's call to the elect.

God is more interested in your calling not your comfort, in your purpose not your preferences.

God is only interested in what He anointed you for, not for what you like and don't like sister.

The Lord stirs up the nest to make you respond to His call. You just get too complacent/comfortable.

Don't let your curiosity about him kill the cat. Just see the cad and be done with him, just like that.

Just knowing/thinking about him holds you down. It's a grey cloud suddenly, a sadness/loss of crown.

WHEN THE HEDGE IS DOWN

WATCH SCENIC DRIVE VIDEOS

After your season of treason full of backstabbing hurts, watch videos on scenic drives for calm first.

The narcissist gave you an up and down life, just when he loved you he dropped you/got new supply.

The narcissistic injuries have been adrenalin-filled and this ugly pattern affected/aged the physical.

Recognize the toll on your body and watch videos of scenic drives. No words, toxic hurt or strife.

Envision you're with parents on vacation. Happy & protected after a trying time neglected/dejected.

BODY RECOMPOSITION

Dried fruit isn't carnivore but it can be HYPER-carnivore. Paleo man ate fruit/didn't count carbs.

The day before your greatest cleansing seems so boring as released crud goes thru the bloodstream.

A Rudderless Ship, Fixed

TORTURED BY FAMILY
IT'S TOO AWFUL, DON'T GO BACK
FAMILY SCAPEGOATS
JESUS WAS *THE* SCAPEGOAT
THE TWO OLDER SISTERS
THE CINDERELLA SYNDROME
ELIMINATING WICKED BANDS
IMPRINTS BY WEIRD RELATIVES
WHAT YOU WENT THRU
PALEO MAN ATE MEAT AND FRUIT
ENCEPHAIZED HEAD/ENLARGED BRAIN
END THOUGHTS

A Rudderless Ship, Fixed

TORTURED BY FAMILY

It's possible to be tortured by your own family. Search "scapegoat" and see the millions of entries.

The myth of family love has kept this silent empire alive for it's denial which prevents healing, aye.

You can avoid outsiders but these people you can't get away from as they squeeze like a python.

The second half of life is the best as these old systems die out and you've relocated to a new nest.

Scapegoats across the world and history, unite! See how common it is and transcend it alright?

Most of life was a black cloud over everything from the bleak reality two older sisters held over me.

But blood is NOT thicker than water. They should be no more important than insults from some joker.

IT'S TOO AWFUL, DON'T GO BACK

You didn't listen to parents so learned the hard way. It was hard time being imposed on like prey.

Don't go back cuz thought loops bring frustration. You made a mistake but learned a helluva lesson.

Thoughts are corrective so we go back to fix it but it's thankless so just thank Him for the self-fix.

In an echo chamber there's no opposition. They only discuss things with those who agree with em.

A RUDDERLESS SHIP, FIXED

See yourself thru your eyes never his, since that varies depending on what distracts him next

FAMILY SCAPEGOATS

Family scapegoats like me are very common and it will take a lifetime to get over it if ever Mom.

The others hop on and the effects are drastic and tragic. Accept they hate you then work magic.

Before accepting they hate you you're always caught in delusion and that's a mental illness son.

Who is that scapegoat? The truth-teller, the empath, the creative one, the aware one are under the gun.

European psychologists call it MOBBING. They all join in, a collusion of weaklings against kings.

It's the Dunning-Kruger Effect: the sad plight of the smart having to adapt to the dumb.

The dumb will catch you in evil webs as bad as their filthy minds can project: I was that kid.

Without family support and feeling betrayed of course, the road is rough until he learns the ropes.

He must stop seeking outer approval and build his own inner reality. That's the solution in finality.

Jesus was hated and He felt it. He expected betrayal. Relate to Him on this, you won't feel suicidal.

JESUS WAS *THE* SCAPEGOAT

Realize Jesus was THE scapegoat and you won't feel so hurt by your family. I know the pain honey.

A RUDDERLESS SHIP, FIXED

If a scapegoat sins as a device to cope, his persecutors will take total control and he's toast.

Women rule their domain thru phone gabbing and reputation-bashing. It's soul murder: calumny.

It is because you're in safety that you're flooded with red hot memories, that's how it works see.

Reaching the end of our endurance is called "hitting bottom". Trauma depletes your ammunition.

THE TWO OLDER SISTERS

You can't fight, you can't do anything as a sheep to the slaughter. Muted, I actually went down that far.

They accept the testimony of the two older sisters against you: the truth-teller, empath or younger.

No judge or jury, what two older sisters said is truth and law, only a few can see the bold treachery.

Because of what I've laid about out women you can understand the cruel Cinderella Syndrome.

The two older women know nothing but their raw power coming from two against one see.

All female power is collusive: they get together with the other broads in their circle and screw ya'.

THE CINDERELLA SYNDROME

Older women hate younger anyway, so getting together becomes solid and permanent treachery.

At death you'll see the entire sequence but for now, just prepare to tell the world what you know.

A RUDDERLESS SHIP, FIXED

Mental illness is being eclipsed by another human being. You're "framed", cut off, censored see.

I coulda walked away and it'd all be ok. But the black cloud follows you--it IS you, this pain.

They "own" you enough to create a bad rep and it's believable as it explodes through gossip.

Calling this up labels you "paranoid" and in some cases mandatory drugging permanently shuts you up.

Female camp guards were the absolute worst/most sadistic. A women's wrath really is cataclysmic.

ELIMINATING WICKED BANDS

Wicked bands are sticky like glue. You have to relocate and eliminate everyone you've talk to.

Once in a new safe life don't let PTSD go on. Just see life as two-pronged ending in victory/freedom.

You were so needy you let em invade your house. Then came your collapse, all due to your guests.

People come and go so worshipping em can get you into a lot of psychic trouble: don't do it friend.

Protect yourself by achieving your own inner reality--who YOU are, even as a child. Nothing else.

Don't let strangers touch you, don't let em in/get into their car. Trust no on but your chosen & the Lord.

People are empty/bored/lonely so drop by to use you for entertainment. Don't EVER allow this.

Tho' the perpetrators are dead and gone, the impact remains and the victim remains forlorned.

A RUDDERLESS SHIP, FIXED

Did your uncle give you trouble? Insight: your beloved father hated him. And thus the picture fills in.

Inherited shame was a big boulder that fell on you, the weakest link in the family crew. That's all Sue.

IMPRINTS BY WEIRD RELATIVES

Weird relatives IMPRINT on a child's brain and it can be a "dying" shame cuz things have really changed.

The good word says you'll be fully satisfied when you wake up to self, so disentrench from this hell.

Himmler seemed like a weak person but turned out to be an evil monster when given authority son.

It's the weak Jolly Jimmy get alongs that become the most tyrannical when given some positions.

Women are ruthless social tacticians: networkers of power while the reclusive, odd girls cower.

WHAT YOU WENT THRU

What you went thru as young woman was horrible but you're here and your perpetrators are in hell now.

It's our unhealed childhood trauma that creates the attraction. It's from chaos and dysfunction.

Attraction to narcissists won't happen if the childhood did not have such chaos and dysfunction.

They specialize in triangulation just to get people fighting as drama is more to their liking.

See past his foibles and realize what you built together and who helped you in stormy weather.

A RUDDERLESS SHIP, FIXED

PALEO MAN ATE MEAT AND FRUIT

If paleo man dried his meat he also dried his fruit. Meat, dried fruit, nuts = perfect 4me too.

If paleo man dried his meat he also dried his fruit. Meat, dried fruit, nuts = perfect for me too.

Meat [easy digestion/no fiber] allowed the enlarged brain as digestive energy shot upward.

Meat heals disease due to the biosimilarity with human tissue & cells. So many health lies this dispels.

ENCEPHAIZED HEAD/ENLARGED BRAIN

The encephalized--enlarged--brain came from less digestive work needed with animal fat/protein.

Apes are mainly fruitarian, their brain remains smaller. Man eats meat also, his brain gets larger.

Not from meat but the digestive energy released due to natural fasting for long periods between.

Fruitarians have to eat all day while carnivores eat then enjoy lengthy periods of creative work/play.

Digestion takes 85% of available energy so this infusion to the brain is enormous and very sexy.

The encephalized head is the "longhead" of nobility vs. squarehead, a sign of satiation and idiocy.

END THOUGHTS

For breathru you gotta be ready. Are you ready? Are you sure, it's a drastic change tho' a jubilee.

Sad Experiences

PEOPLE WANNA PEG YOU
IT'S EASIEST TO BEGIN AGAIN
NO PAIN WASTE
THE WAIT IS THE TEST
HE HATES YOU FOR LEAVING
A BREATH OF FRESH AIR
HE'LL ALWAYS WANT ANOTHER
GOD IS THE WAYMAER
END THOUGHTS

Sad Experiences

PEOPLE WANNA PEG YOU

Starting all over again in a new town brings instant relief: It's due to social psychology I think.

People wanna peg you and once pegged they'll fill their cup with it and never/EVER forget.

Rather than living it down, relocation is the cure 99% of the time. God forgives but they don't, yikes.

The contagion of madness is the stickiness of socially-driven insanity and popular narratives.

IT'S EASIEST TO BEGIN AGAIN

It's just easier to begin again, to wipe the slate clean. God will put you where He wants you see.

Of course paleo man ate the brightly colored fruit on trees [more like a drink] in addition to meat.

Before meeting a narcissist you're a bright, happy shining star which they turn into dust.

Peter says if you want peace you gotta seek & pursue it. There's an obstruction against privacy, I knew it.

God put me in painful experiences to write about em. Also to learn so it never/EVER happens again.

He's always gonna act that way with other women, so curb your biggest enemy: your imagination.

SAD EXPERIENCES

NO PAIN WASTE

Pain of bad experience is never wasted. "No pain waste": like how Jesus' death has impacted.

The pain of temporary challenges always makes us stronger and more resilient, we know this.

The pain of the past was part of the inevitable process. We go through pain and end in success.

I was no longer so resentful of past actors when I saw the inevitable process of DOWN then UP.

There's no pain waste nor time waste, for everything's in it's proper sequence as God allows it.

People leaving your life is a sign of assured success soon. Many panic at this change, so inopportune.

To complete your journey and get what you want you must WAIT. This is so hard many give up ok.

THE WAIT IS THE TEST

The WAIT is your test. Many lose faith and try to force success. After completion just wait, that's best.

The wait is maturing you to perfection. Completion of your work was actually just the beginning.

Give up all that work, obstacles, all that pain--for nothing? Don't you want what you're deserving?

Hang in there, don't give up now. Get the goodies for all your good works. The WAIT is the last course.

The function of a spouse is to be the ONE person who doesn't leave--God says we need just one see.

SAD EXPERIENCES

The bible says we'll always have one good friend so that's your beloved home for now, amen.

HE HATES YOU FOR LEAVING

He hates you for leaving because the narcissist will NEVER see what he did to bring it on darling.

He did egregious/horrible things to you but cuz he'd never acknowledge em you forgave the fool.

If people won't acknowledge their faults then the justified reaction is driven in til you're nuts.

If he never acknowledges he did anything wrong then the onus falls on YOU: you're the problem.

The narc will always idealize then discard, he'll always use petty approval tactics with the girls.

He will always get bored and need new diversions with new/other women. It's endless with this man.

She finally gets the gumption to leave and he acts surprised anyone could leave HIM see.

A BREATH OF FRESH AIR

It hurts so much adapting to his narc style that leaving is a breath of fresh air never felt before, aye.

You want a reliable man who pays the bills. It's as simple as that, it's not too much to ask still.

A nice man will bring you emotional stability, freeing up an incredible amount of creative energy.

Adaptating to a flashy phony will shut down your creative energy as you sink in your swill honey.

SAD EXPERIENCES

A nice man is a stable man, no ups/downs, hot/cold. For the first time you feel secure in your home.

If he's an alcoholic it's ups/downs and humiliations. I couldn't take it and chose a higher station.

If he's a gigolo like a boy in your house, always soaking you dry, eject this parasite and delouse.

If he's asking you for money, reject this phony. Never respect men who do this, how weasely.

Just because he begs you back doesn't mean he's gonna change or be any better for you: fact.

HE'LL ALWAYS WANT ANOTHER

Just cuz the narc moves on to someone else doesn't mean he'll leave you alone, he wants it all.

Someone lives a life that is fabulously great then he ages/dies and someone else takes his place.

It feels so good to get outa his influence. When you no longer have to filter things thru his highness.

To be mad at people in this generation means you're mad all the time so it's best to be stoic, aye.

You had to go thru pain but pain is never wasted. For wisdom & success it's even an investment.

Don't complain ok for you never went to jail, were never in a war and were never kidnapped or raped.

Much worse things have happened to people. Lessen PTSD by seeing the universality of human evil.

GOD IS THE WAYMAER

SAD EXPERIENCES

My God's a waymaker. Whenever you don't see a way you know God is there, a solution engineer.

You've finished your work and now face the abyss that nothing's happening with it: ask God sis.

God's answers are beyond clever, thing's you'd NEVER think of yourself. He's a total genius, my Father.

God's a social engineer. He can fix any relation tho' it's hit bottom, caused destruction, gone nuclear.

I'm ashamed for every time Satan used me. But God said I'd never be condemned cuz it's erased see.

You HAD to go no-contact cuza how he treated you so now he's stuck but sorry, that's his bad luck.

I completely forgive you to be free of you, you little weasel/demon/little man and ogre scrooge.

END THOUGHTS

The Way-Maker, Miracle Worker, Promise Keeper, Light in the Darkness: that is Who You Are.

He makes a way where there is no way: imagine that! He keeps His promises and ejects dirty rats.

The WAIT is based on pure faith on things unseen and thus it's a necessary part of the process see.

The wait isn't hard knowing He's a waymaker, miracle-worker and promise-keeper--it'll be a lark.

Realize that continuous guilt/shame are not from God but Satan. Sins are erased by death of His Son.

The WAIT brings your maturation to perfection though at the time it feels like excruciating frustration.

SAD EXPERIENCES

Are you ready to go worldwide on camera? No? Then why are you begging for this: prepare more.

Can you be exposed to scrutiny, is there anything hidden, have you weeded your friendship garden?

When out of office they still run the country, when in office they expand non-elected parties.

Conspiracy theorists are just pattern-recognitionists. We see this and know it immediately sis.

"I laid sad experiences before you to write about it"--the Lord. And I said "it was a pleasure to serve."

Keys to a Short Life

BE TRUE TO SELF AND GOD
ALL GOD'S TIMING
PERSECUTION SHAPED YOU
SMALL MINDS AND OLD BATS
SMALL TOWN/MIND NEUROSIS
A SCARY SITUATION
QUEEN BEE AND FLYING MONKEYS
SEASON OF TREASON
MEMORIES OF THE LOWER RUNG
AVOID RECKLESS BOYS!
THE FEMININE SET UP/MINDSET
CREEPS CREEPING INTO HOUSES
THE UNFINISHED EXES
TRUST NO MAN WITH BLURRED LINES

Keys to a Short Life

The key to a short life is to disregard God. People perish from lack of His wisdom or the rod.

My goal is to make you independent, i.e. less enmeshed in human systems holding you down or nuts.

You must relocate to escape people's misperceptions, accusations and collective put downs.

BE TRUE TO SELF AND GOD

Don't allow someone's lack of boundaries impose on your need for privacy. It comes first you see.

You lost your soul talking that way and brought disgust from people who mattered and it's not ok.

My young brain felt amorphous as dust, I didn't know who I was and had been hurt in love.

Don't blame the stupid cruelty of people. Your hedge being down it was principalities & powers/evil.

You're not walking away from abusive actors so much as your season of treason/era of bad luck.

ALL GOD'S TIMING

Destiny snatched me outa my tiny cabin and put me in a mansion. It's all in God's timing my son.

You pay your dues, and there was a lot I had to pay off. Then suddenly one day it's over/I had to laugh.

KEYS TO A SHORT LIFE

When your lessons were done, the bad season was over and God took you away to your reward.

What were those lessons? Being around crazy snotty evil people then writing 120 books about em.

He gave me sad experiences to write about em. It was a pleasure to serve Lord, now let's go on.

Let go of petty sin memories and enter the wide expansion--unless reminded by your friends.

God gave me sad experiences for wisdom but never intended me to hang onto them, amen.

The camp prison guards were all arrested and hung and now you're onto a brand new life hon'.

All that pain and loneliness will never be wasted. You're light years ahead of other due to this sis.

PERSECUTION SHAPED YOU

All that persecution for uniqueness shaped you in a certain way and the Potter reflected it ok.

God hates false accusers. These are masters at sly innuendo, the backstab reputation busters.

Being a victim of malicious gossip will make you an expert in social psychology on the way up.

Being targeted by malicious sisters will make you an expert in life and a lady of substance later.

Waking up to people makes you an expert all around since it's life, destiny and time you've found.

You've gotten back the time & energy allotted to human dramas. You're impervious with new stamina.

KEYS TO A SHORT LIFE

Transcend petty pecking orders and have universal power and creativity of great discoverers.

Let local gossip pull you down or TRANSCEND the petty parochial to achieve higher global renown?

Get hung up on past actors or let go and go on to wider perception with more universal adulation?

SMALL MINDS AND OLD BATS

Small minds can be cruel as they can't take in your kind. Persecution's painful/hard to take, aye.

A victim of small minds feels he wants to run and hide. All cuz his haters trash all outside their line.

The old bats in the neighborhood kept me humble [thorns in my side] 'til God put my in view.

The old bats were the Potter's wheel in maturing me full. Cuz I never listened to mom/found her dull.

I grew to fear old women the most. Old can be evil--people don't always get nice with age you know.

The old bats in the neighborhood kept me humble [thorns in my side] 'til God ended ALL troubles.

The old bats misjudge everything you do. Their dark minds project their crap onto you--PeeU!

I couldn't believe the things they said about me. They're psychotic, dumbed down, puny.

SMALL TOWN/MIND NEUROSIS

It was horrors living in small town/mind neurosis but in the end probably a good thing perhaps.

KEYS TO A SHORT LIFE

Commingling with small minds I was always stamping out fires. Often explaining myself, embarrassed.

It's not about the small town, just how independent you are. It's the social thing that makes it war.

Commingling with small minds I was always stamping out fires. Often explaining myself—not a liar.

It's the Dunning-Kruger effect of the smart adapting to the dumb who has tyranny over us: no fun!

All to show off to certain people you made an ass of yourself to the whole world. Think, girl!

As much as I disliked her I always knew she was over there--that is the function of a neighbor.

A SCARY SITUATION

It's scary since you can't make em understand you, they don't have the capacity to. Relocate, whew.

When mobbed by dumb all you can do is stay mum. You can't make em self-aware geniuses son.

Oh, to be accused by small minds, is there anything worse? It brings out your best or you're toast.

I'm gonna tell you something you never heard before: the dumb are mean, the smart more accepting.

Does she deserve your compassion and forgiveness? She's playing a role/too social/it's ridiculous.

Forgive him but don't forget hon'. Yet you're trauma-bonding instead, and with a mean bum?

QUEEN BEE AND FLYING MONKEYS

KEYS TO A SHORT LIFE

Queen Bee goes right to the head of the women's social group. That's how the dumb broads rule.

She makes her [wanna-bes] flying monkeys enforcers against girls the she-bully doesn't like see.

Small addicted minds are the most closed down and that is most prevalent in a tiny liberal town.

They will NOT let you live your life even tho' they say they do. Officious, gossipy, catty shrews.

Virtue signaling is not goodness but she will never see this. Unable to change she implodes sis.

SEASON OF TREASON

They can't help their small/mean minds. All men are sinners but dumb anger you can't temper.

The point is to let it go: to forgive others, forget the actors and see it all as principalities and powers.

He rains on your parade and takes the wind out of your sails. Every time you go there it's a fail.

All things work together for lovers of God so you never wasted pain/time, it made you a power rod.

It's not just a viewpoint if it's demonstrably false but they won't listen to facts or anything else.

MEMORIES OF THE LOWER RUNG

You were on the lower rung in your treason season but you don't have to worry about it repeatin'.

Your only problem now is memory. PTSD from being treated as subhuman like in wars see.

KEYS TO A SHORT LIFE

A woman must never chase a man due to her emotional construction not allowing rejection.

Men learn in barber shops how to manage a woman's psychology. lovebomb, grow cold, control.

Break her down, break her down into the ground, control her until she's dumbed.

He lovebombs so completely then recedes, she chases him to recapture that old sweetie: please!

The feminine soul of woman is not designed to process rejection or deferred hope: treachery.

AVOID RECKLESS BOYS!

Girls, avoid those reckless boys who make foolish decisions and wanna involve you in them.

Women are thirsty for love as men are for sex. From that comes misery for the female like a hex.

Built into her is an innate desire for intimacy and loyal connection to the right man, not rejection.

When he gets her to open up and love, she's emotionally compromised like hand in glove.

A man is compromised by sex with strange women: physically weakened. A woman, just by lovin'.

And thus the negative impact of soul ties is seen in women to a much greater degree than men.

When a woman loves a man she's immediately put in the position where he can break her see.

He can now break her if she's not conscious--if she's not intentional. You gotta be aware of this gal.

KEYS TO A SHORT LIFE

I was one big giant wound. I was so prickly the world came back worse at me, the doomed.

My describing the systems people suddenly see what they couldn't before and escape this war.

Because of her set up connecting to this man will produce a pain unfathomable, I recall it well.

The woman is engineered to desire the approval and acceptance of her man. Just think of that.

THE FEMININE SET UP & MINDSET

The woman is engineered to desire approval & acceptance of her man--as vulnerable as that.

With the wrong man, the desire of the woman is twisted into an emotional web, a trap of bedlam.

First he's her knight in shining armor then he pulls back into continuous cold rejection of her.

Trap # 1: When a man makes her chase him only to reject her. More broken, more he controls her.

Trap #2: Letting him move in. Maid, cook, bed partner: he wants his "crib" which is for babies, amen.

CREEPS CREEPING INTO HOUSES

Only creeps creep into houses leading sinful females astray. They are without boundaries ok.

I don't want em coming here for the bathroom or charging phones. I'm not a gas station I'm a home.

She's a woman without limits who lets a man in her door. Instantly she's lost all her power.

KEYS TO A SHORT LIFE

It's a lot easier to let the devil in then to kick him out. Another thing: don't get in his car/truck.

It's easier to get possessed than it is to be exorcised. You gotta teach kids this: resist the evil guy.

Letting a man in your house gives him space to create an emotional, financial or spiritual soul tie ok.

THE UNFINISHED EXES

Trap # 3: "Complicated" ex status. It's a red flag for a man to not clear up former exes before you sis.

He's either confused or running game on you and the ex: he's sleeping with both of you chix.

This downward spiral from common traps can degrade a woman's identity for decades, by rats.

People get divorced and still stay in the bed, so sleeping with both is a very common thread.

You never realized you were part of a trio 'til years later but it's still a disgusting thing sister.

You were part of a harem, a stable of women and you didn't even know it. Ha ha ha, imagine that.

Loving a man who can't make a decision: the doubleminded are unstable in all their ways man.

TRUST NO MAN WITH BLURRED LINES

How can you trust a man with so many blurred lines? Are you that gullible yet to be so refined?

A man with unclear ex status heavily pursuing you and you're biting on the bait: this is unconscious.

KEYS TO A SHORT LIFE

Trap #4: You're in love with a man in a totally private affair--with no public acknowledgement sister?

Hey Boss Chick: why are you a secret? This is a slap in the face and it's because you put up with it.

Why settle for being a secret--something shameful and hidden? Are you not insulted and saddened?

Think: heaven, then there is no past. But Einstein said this too when "what is eternity?" he asked.

Season of Treason

SEASON OF TREASON
KEEP EM OUT AND RELAX
TRAUMA KEEPS YOU HOOKED
COURAGE IS FORWARD MOTION
EVIL GOSSIP AND DIVISION
FALSE BRETHREN
PRIDE
GOD'S WRATH ON ENEMIES
COVERT NARCISSISM
PROVERBS SAYS IT

Season of Treason

SEASON OF TREASON

It was your season of treason and meant to build muscle. No reason to have PTSD, just go on now.

No one understood your pain and they all went on his side. I remember the season so well, aye.

I had no boundaries or felt need for protection so God brought evil boys in to teach me my lessons.

Inferiors got involved just to bring you down. You lost all privacy and felt like a slave, not renowned.

It's a season when nothing works out, you're blamed for it all, they avoid you and gossip like you're odd.

Lose your privacy, lose your power as you gotta adapt to others and the devil wants to devour.

He put me in a den of devils so I could learn about, overcome and write it out for you all.

KEEP EM OUT AND RELAX

To rest in your femininity you must be strong enough to not let em break you down, from after ur born.

It's easy to get into a war but hard to get out. Catastrophic changes and you're stuck.

You have evil forebodings: Fear/anxiety over the next disaster since it's all you've known so far sir.

Fear and anxiety are from Satan too. Confront him: he's not gonna steal what Jesus died to give you.

SEASON OF TREASON

Emptiness is a very deep childhood wound: from not feeling seen, heard or understood too.

Life is a ladder. It's conflicts on the bottom rung but as you progress you never experience em again.

The bad won't repeat itself unless YOU fall back to the lower rungs, taking the lesson all over again.

TRAUMA KEEPS YOU HOOKED

He creates trauma in you since that keeps you engaged. His supply is your fear, sadness or rage.

Narcissists survive off our emotional reactions to: trauma, devaluation, character assassination.

ALL of your ups and downs are designed to take you where you need to be. ALL OF IT honey.

Self-defense is written in my DNA now but it took years of invasions to see a need to build this wall.

The daughter of a narcissistic mother goes thru the worst experiences known to mankind sir.

COURAGE IS FORWARD MOTION

Courage is forward motion while you feel afraid. God pushes our limits, we do it then it's all ok.

Had I tried to be popular with people I would not now be an apostle of the Lord Jesus Christ. Paul

Trauma bond wears off, you see him truly and wonder how you ever coulda been so foolish.

Relax, it'll never happen again cuz you're higher now. You've progressed, that was down/low.

SEASON OF TREASON

Work/sacrifice produces much better results than just hopping around from spouse to spouse.

Bad associations will be a trojan horse to wreak havoc in your life. Stay away or feel hellish strife.

Avoid evil influences for bad company corrupts good manners and concession leads to compromise.

Avoid false teachers by testing spirits–from God? You are to avoid em not reform em thru your "love".

EVIL GOSSIP AND DIVISION

Get away from divisive spirits. Don't become party to destructive gossip for curiosity kills cats.

These people have only one goal in mind: to bring division. They can't stop relationship killin'

He brings evil gossip and stirs up division. After a brief warning, have nothing more to do with him.

The bible says such a person is warped and sinful. He himself is self-condemned–I figured so.

He brought accusatory, inquiring, evil gossip about me and I told him never to come here again see.

I told him I didn't even know the man. They intend to bring you down/break the queen/create bedlam.

With divisive gossip and unfair comparisons your mind and self-esteem is brought right down.

FALSE BRETHREN

Christians who profess but don't confess: avoid the sexually immoral, the greedy or idolatrous.

SEASON OF TREASON

Reviler, drunkard, swindler: Avoid and don't try to love em into goodness cuz it won't work sister.

Silently thank enemies for the trouble and persecution coo, for it built necessary muscle in thee.

God said not even to eat with such a one--how more clear could it be to avoid dividers/bums?

PRIDE

Avoid proud people. PRIDE is a badge of honor in our society but we're to be humble as pride is evil.

Those who exalt themselves are humbled under the mighty hand of God. For the proud, watch out.

You're just as bad if you get swept up with the puffed up prideful powers so stay humble/pure.

Watch men who creep into female households to capture weak women with sins of their own.

The men are prideful, feeling entitled. And the women aren't humble or they'd realize the danger still.

The women are led astray by various passions, ever learning but never coming to truth son.

The world is growing more coldhearted and narcissistic but for your inner circle, avoid these twits.

Why? They'll be a trojan horse to bring down your life causing havoc, lost reputation and strife.

Follow the biblical command to STAY AWAY but at the very least, guard your heart my sweetest.

You're a hardworking, kind and humble person. You deserve more than hassle and contradiction.

SEASON OF TREASON

Your love can't change a narcissist so attend to God's signs when He says give up on someone sis.

Remember, there are those God commands you stay away from. You know em, the world's full of em.

Substitute gratitude for what you've got rather than resentments of those who don't love God.

When you bear much fruit you prove yourselves to be my disciples and glorify my Father. John 15

GOD'S WRATH ON ENEMIES

All I thought about was getting back or "why didn't I say this or that". My present perception was flat.

Let God take care of the enemy, and He WILL as I have proven through my many days with glee.

He put them down and me in a new land. I don't wanna waste one more minute thinking of them.

"I have broken the teeth of the ungodly". Hah: when I saw him again he was a toothless tragedy.

Abusive men perish/abusive women are widowed, you see things looking back, that's all I know.

Entrust both your success and enemies to God. You're his child: He vindicates/protects His own.

God's wrath is fire coming outa His nostrils. It's the Kings bringing us down that He's gonna kill.

Tyranny: Opposition will ramp up but they'll keep doing what they do cuz insanity can't stop.

It's harder to disprove the New World Order than it is to prove it in 2023. We all know about tyranny.

SEASON OF TREASON

All are dumbed down save a few who see what's happening. It's a scary time, very challenging.

COVERT NARCISSISM

A covert narcissist isn't an in-your-face grandiose jerk you can spot right away--he's subtle/indirect.

A covert is passive-aggressive so you're the only one seeing the damage he does which is massive.

No judge or jury, they assume it's all true. It's frightening to be in a culture/family of fools.

He may be helpful and unassuming, very considerate of others. He helps children, the elderly, neighbors.

This poser cares about everyone but you. He couldn't care less about your needs, feelings, views.

A narc needs multiple sources of supply to keep living, not getting approval from themselves see.

PROVERBS SAYS IT

When it goes well with the righteous the city rejoices, when the wicked perish, shouts of gladness.

Whoever slanders reveals secrets, but the trustworthy in spirit keeps the thing covered--he's correct.

Maintaining confidences strengthens relationships but a big mouth always ends it [who needs it?]

He who trusts in riches will fall but the righteous flourish like the green leaf: it's not all money see.

He who troubles his own household will inherit the wind. I suppose I did that way back then.

SEASON OF TREASON

He who troubles his own household will inherit the wind. I suppose I did that way back then.

The fool will be servant to the wise at heart. That guy's been an embarrassment from the start.

If righteous are repaid on earth, how much more the wicked and sinner? They perish/die in the gutter.

Signs you should leave: He treats you poorly. Stop being a burden bearer or a sin enabler.

Don't allow your mind to run through it over and over again. Instead say: get behind me Satan.

Satan's armory is all our mistakes from birth. He's got a lot of ammunition, only If we let him of course.

END THOUGHTS 2023

You can't make people be smart/understand you. That's the frustrating thing, you're screwed.

Carnivore: removing inflammatory foods while adding nutrient dense which are uninflammatory too.

Deluded Friends and Globalist Authoritarians

BOUNDARY SMASHING
YOU KNEW HE WAS A THIEF
GUEST HATRED
BASHING BOUNDARIES
EMOTIONAL HOT BUTTONS
WHEN GOD SHUTS OFF THE HEART
THE ADDICTION TO INSTABILITY
WICKED HUMAN BANDS
THE DUMBED IN DENIAL
DELUDED FRIENDS
MAL-ADAPT TO STUPID CRAP
NARCISSISTIC PARENTS
WOMEN'S RAGES
GLOBALIST AUTHORITARIANS

Deluded Friends and Globalist Authoritarians

BOUNDARY SMASHING

The narc will smash all boundaries, assuming everything including the kid's thoughts see.

Ongoing invasions of privacy and boundary violations: I was a cat in a roomful of rockingchairs son.

Then later I'd let invaders into my home and they crushed my boundaries into the ground.

I was mad about it and sought to avoid it but could not stand up against it by saying "GET OUT".

Letting em in went against my deepest objections and this contradiction created PTSD bedlam.

People's invasions were excruciating pain to my psyche but I needed em to change my trajectory.

Men who didn't even deserve a conversation were let in to ask invasive demeaning questions.

Things got so bad I bottomed out on people and realized my desire for solitude/hatred of evil.

Think about it: they come into YOUR house and impose their crap on you. That's TOO CLOSE too.

YOU KNEW HE WAS A THIEF

Don't blame the thief because you knew he was a thief. Blame yourself for letting evil in see.

DELUDED FRIENDS & AUTHORITARIANS

There comes a time when you leave the narc. God is protecting His child by turning off your heart.

They wanna use you/let all their friends use you too. It's a hard realization about the human zoo.

It's like me putting a rattlesnake in my house then complaining of the stress and death.

I had yet to learn that--war games in a man's world--so I thank my foes for helping me to develop.

Tell him: you're a dirty cheater and I'm not gonna do it to her. Don't call me again or I'll tell her.

GUEST HATRED

Hatred of one's guests: their oughta be a word for it, the bible says we grow to despise the pests.

A man's foot is too much into your house! That's what the word says re: hatred of uninvited guests.

They don't have a life and you do, they are energy vampires. They'll drop in if you let em sir.

I thank those cheap grifters who taught me these precious lessons about the sick humans.

They are gremlins, sparks in the night that perish outa sight: lemmings, the whole tribe suicides.

Don't let em into your home. They are taught the social is more important than a brain of your own.

The mob will thus destroy/steal everything you own and devalue your wonderful godly goals.

After they devastate your life don't come back to me wailing for you let em in with their mobbing.

DELUDED FRIENDS & AUTHORITARIANS

Now you're gonna have PTSD from what you allowed to happen by letting them in like a dunce son.

Let your slogan be: Nip it in the Bud. Don't let it go on because then they expect it like cats & dogs.

BASHING BOUNDARIES

If your invaders/guests don't know the real YOU they'll be bashing your boundaries constantly too.

A narc mother's disrespect for boundaries leads to that child's accepting invasion from others see.

Transient relationships lack depth and understanding. It's scary, that's why I always preferred privacy.

Standing up for myself only made things worse. Comply quickly to avoid confrontation first.

Submit or be rejected at the expense of self-expression or ever feeling sovereign and respected.

The parent will exploit a kid's successes but never give support and love which most require sis.

A narc parent knows each child's emotional triggers and uses guilt, fear and other tactics sir.

A parent knows exactly the buttons to push for he installed them as his punishments.

EMOTIONAL HOT BUTTONS

Emotional "hot" buttons and issues are pressed whenever they want, just think about it.

The victim child is thus programmed to be easily manipulated but you must resist hon'.

DELUDED FRIENDS & AUTHORITARIANS

If you can't say "NO!" you'll be six feet under cuz they'll take everything you own and more.

The victim allows others to use these buttons and vulnerabilities against them: so sad, amen.

Narc parents play favorites and pit one against the other. Two against a weak one? even better.

WHEN GOD SHUTS OFF THE HEART

When your heart turns off for the narc you have no more feeling--a normal sign of God's saving.

God's had enough of your heart being burned over and over so He's turned off the spigot of you lover.

God has protected you by shutting off your heart. It's time for you and your heart to leave the narc.

If God has turned off your heart towards bad association, get down on your knees and thank Him.

When God turns off hot obsession you feel a sudden lightening, happiness after cold depression.

"I felt so happy not thinking of him constantly. i saw his picture and he meant nothing." Lady

Suddenly a brand new vista opens up, free of the black cloud of continuous disappointments.

THE ADDICTION TO INSTABILITY

Involvements with unstable people becomes horrendous addiction: the stickiness of Satan.

One way or another there's always a problem but the word says we'll always one good friend.

DELUDED FRIENDS & AUTHORITARIANS

I'm happy with one chosen friend or mate, not a roundtable discussion with anonymous face.

Looking back it was hell. They were dumb but totally in control. How to reconcile this was my role.

WICKED HUMAN BANDS

Human bands are wicked and sticky especially in the social game of who's superior to who ok.

Coming under their control you submerge/lose your own reality and this is the sickening scene ok.

At this point your trusted friend reverts to side with the enemy against you. Your reality splits in two.

People side with the perceived in power. When you were dethroned you saw your allies sour.

Thus the shifting sands of human systems: They either lock, constantly re-align or someone kills em.

When down no one wants any association with you. They disavow you publicly [socially screwed].

It's the Fallen Hero Syndrome: whereas they loved you now they wanna kill you on the way down.

Refugees of this process know Social Psychology very well. It's about the herd and it's predictable.

A stigma is formed that is impossible to extinguish. The kings of the earth wanna bring us down sis.

There's this constant undertow. I could always feel it which is why I always wanted to be alone.

THE DUMBED IN DENIAL

DELUDED FRIENDS & AUTHORITARIANS

Before someone knows, they don't know. It's a red pill sudden change after being blind to the foe.

You can't do a thing before their conversion. They're in the dark and arrogant in ignorance son.

A deep thinker is in continual state of terror until he learns to constantly & daily cast his care.

Seeing all the implications and ramifications is depleting so he puts it in God's hands daily.

The superior man figures out exactly what he has control over/what he doesn't, then does it.

Pinpoint daily: what's in the works, what's been done and waiting to flower, what to tackle today.

DELUDED FRIENDS

A deluded friend thinks you're inferior for your views and they arrogantly reject it all: pee-yew

These friends who are still deluded, they're gonna avoid you anyway so just let em go and be renewed.

Your deluded friends arrogantly reject your input as if it's inferior, mad or obscene [it's mean].

A deep thinker is hurt by deluded friends so I'd choose solitude for some time and thank God, amen.

Once you've cast your care on God, your only Friend, don't repeat it over again or it's like chanting.

Your mother was a slanderer miss. she liked Warren AKA Pocahontas and Bernie, a communist.

Not one of them asked me if it was true. They all just assumed: no judge or jury, I was the shrew.

DELUDED FRIENDS & AUTHORITARIANS

Your therapy is to look at gorgeous mansions all day while listening to your favorite music ok.

Envision yourself in that new role so your reactions to the universe change making it all possible.

It's not that you're creating your reality as new agers say, but you're filling in the dots that way.

MAL-ADAPT TO STUPID CRAP

The fact is they are stupider than you so they could lock you up if you don't figure a way out soon.

Stupid cruelty: this exists and will be your reality. If you don't garner respect expect raw treachery.

It was just a few events but they shaped my entire life and were recalled a million times, yikes.

He is a predatory parasite: he will take everything that you have and live off of you if he can, aye.

A narcissist wants social approval/seeks undeserved status but I'd rather work for mine thanks.

Just the mere fact that you were going through it shows you still had the lesson to learn doesn't it?

One lost his teeth, one lost his eyesight and one his mind. Eventually it all evens up, aye.

The less you do the more you get done. It's a case of less is more: the power of leisure and fun.

I always sensed a gathering of fools around sir but then some just seemed much wiser than others.

Once free of protective home I felt hit from all sides and sought only good foundation, never to roam.

DELUDED FRIENDS & AUTHORITARIANS

NARCISSISTIC PARENTS

A mature person is simply someone who's learned how NOT to be controlled by others/no favors.

Narc parents are jealous of their children and show competitive behavior that's mean and rotten.

Narc parents give mean insults in public and microaggressions to bash them down quick.

The child is being undermined psychologically. Parents frustrating their kids do Satan's job see.

I felt I was inherently defective causing me to deserve such treatment, even with all knowing it.

By constantly demeaning a child it forces them to rely on outer validation and approval for life.

Needing approval means meeting other's "needs" while ignoring our own. Sexual favors full blown.

Narc parents feel entitled to violate a kid's boundaries and they gossip about him to their cronies.

I had no identity, it was "repeat after me". All I knew was from a young age I wanted to be alone see.

WOMEN'S RAGES

It wasn't my dad, he was as scared as me soon. He'd lock himself in his bedroom every afternoon.

There are raging females across the land, fueled by alcohol and the feminist narrative/global plan.

"I am furious" was Cindy's favorite phrase. I heard it every day and it was always justified ok.

DELUDED FRIENDS & AUTHORITARIANS

They always feel justified/have a right to assert their bombastic authority—they HAVE to see.

Women you got the husband and kids so scared of your rages and it's NOT God's plan for the ages.

Abortions cause "unexplained" rages towards the mate. You don't get off Scot free from your fate.

It's still not as bad as women targeting each other. This gets so dirty only relocation is the answer.

Rage: the anti-female spirit. We're to be gentle, tender and loving but regarding sin raise kids to fear it.

GLOBALIST AUTHORITARIANS

There are terrorist organizations pretending to be governments. They'll kill a million in a minute.

Look at the millions who died for Hitler. Such terrorists think nothing of sacrificing other humans sir.

We could all be hit by acts of government terrorism thru fires, hurricanes, outages onto their target.

Water everywhere but not a drop to drink. There's no more satisfaction in this world I think.

They don't believe it cuz they don't wanna believe it. That's how shallow your friends are, forget it.

Veganism as new age theory destroys immunity. Protein deprivation also ages skin/drains energy.

Hypercarnivore: 80% meat, 20% fruit, nuts, butter, yogurt, cream, cheese. No plants or grains ever see.

They won't care until it hits their door, lulled into la la land through CNN and other media whores.

DELUDED FRIENDS & AUTHORITARIANS

The biggest taboo of our times is the joint identity of people of European heritage: white guys.

I'm not a white supremacist, I'm a tribalist. I think all groups wanna hang with their own I'll bet.

Maui: don't give em water, don't trim the trees, leave the power on, barricade the exit, no siren.

He who is not angry when there's just cause for anger is immoral because anger serves justice.

They weren't Christians, just angry authoritarians from a false church and they didn't go to heaven.

God's the Waymaker so just do your work and relax all day. You can't make it happen, there's no way.

The root of the righteous shall never be moved so just keep doing what you're doing I behoove.

THE UNDERTOW

WE'RE ALL UNIQUE
WORK AGAINST THE UNDERTOW
POSSESSED BY LOWER AFFECTIONS
DON'T SWEAT YOUR BAD REP
THE TYRANNY OF MADWOMEN
NARCISSIST PARENTS
PEOPLE MADE ME SICK
ANTI-FEMALE SPIRIT
NO PRIVACY IN BEDLAM
FURIOUS FEMALES
BREAKTHROUGH IS FROM GOD
DONALD TRUMP AND POPULISM

THE UNDERTOW

WE'RE ALL UNIQUE

You think things no one has ever thought before. You add to the human library and it's unique sir.

Every species has its genotype and genius is ours as we co-create with God receptive to the stars.

They found me strange and I didn't know how to deal with it. I felt despicable because of this.

Due to ostracism I attached too quickly to men for protection in a low calibration of mate-selection.

I was different on every level and fit in nowhere so wrote 121 books to show a mental way far better.

See the benefits of horrible bad days. Trouble makes you stoic and betrayal gives you discernment.

WORK AGAINST THE UNDERTOW

Girl: you gotta be your own encourager. Talk to yourself as a parent to a child and especially, love her.

Cuz the perverted male world seeks to break her down from birth. You gotta work against this girl.

A man only loves a queen but men in general break us down so we can never obtain that status see.

I felt this undertow whenever around people. I just wanted to be alone from when a little girl.

THE UNDERTOW

Any sign of independence was quickly squashed and I brought notice with my utterances, bashed.

When alone I felt I could conquer the universe but when with people all hopes were dashed/cursed.

It was a constant swing between megalomania and severe low self-esteem. This was not a queen.

I sought their approval but they could also pull the rug out. I was not mentally sovereign like now.

If needing approval God may remove IT ALL. Then you're forced to just seek His: windfall!

There comes a time in every narcissist's life when he realizes he can't fake it anymore, aye.

POSSESSED BY LOWER AFFECTIONS

I know what it's like being possessed by a lower affection: food, sex, drugs, booze, gamblin'.

Before being free of afflictions one cannot "see". Mostly, it's impossible to reach his destiny.

You will not have breakthru if stuck in old sins. These youthful follies gotta go, THEN you show.

I know, my mom gossiped about me too. But that was a different era and we're about to BREAKTHRU.

This time of WAITING will not go on forever. Could be today you'll get a visitation and then power.

The point is: how do you wait? For this is the test in God's eyes, when it's based on pure faith.

You keep looking for cues, for "likes" or any indication that you're making a mark or even exist, yikes!

THE UNDERTOW

You're hidden under God's wings--your light under a bushel--until **HE** reveals His kings/queens.

Cruel: that's how they are with status--tension & aggression but you're **God's** son so hell with em.

You just gotta be happy on the lower rungs then God gives you the high life, from shack to mansion.

WAIT: We're all waiting for something and hopefully it's an elevation from where we are see.

When down there it's all about status tension & aggression and establishing boundaries son.

DON'T SWEAT YOUR BAD REP

Don't sweat your bad rep for it was **LIBERALS** causing the problem and we didn't deserve all that.

You're just a name and a rumor. As your archetype changes no one believes it anyway sir.

They have no lines going along with anything except **YOU** about whom they gossip constantly.

Going no contact includes online. No going there or lurking--spying: he's banished from your mind.

The women in cop encounters never had a dad to curb them. They bark like animals/bedlam.

Crude and gross: they never had sane & sober parents to refine them. They're whorish too ma'am.

They're drunk. I recalled as a youth I was drunk much of the time and gave no thought to it, aye.

They have no lines and are outa their mind. They're drunk too and entitled so fence up now, aye.

THE UNDERTOW

The female spirit--meant to be loving/tender--has become the opposite and that is a sadist.

With tenacity of a bulldog she targets you with a permanent grudge. All you can do is call on God.

THE TYRANNY OF MADWOMEN

I saw her as a madwoman. I learned to laugh as the only way to keep myself from being broken.

Caricaturing the tyrant is a way of mocking and it blunts the attacks. The truth is I lost all respect.

The anti-female spirit is a hater. It feels good to hate and gossip runs the war like a third grader.

Mom is a narcissistic raging alcoholic. Who's she got but her daughter to go full on lunatic?

Her issue is "get him/her back". She'll get her cronies to do it and you won't know what hit you Mack.

Homicidal impulses towards the mother turn into suicidal/self-destructive actions in the future.

Suddenly she recalled wanting to kill mom at five. That brought a FLOOD of fear she had of that dyke.

Angry women hating/rejected by men: that's not a good role model to have as a mother friend.

NARCISSIST PARENTS

The girl's first bully was her mom putting her down, priming her for the narcissist later on.

To the parent the child is "too sensitive", thus downplaying his emotions & feelings to himself.

THE UNDERTOW

Something that happened only once they say is a regular pattern: in gossip is expansion.

A scapegoat in the system goes through a meat grinder and comes out a recluse, a happy-at-homer.

Like a crisis in nature suddenly the whole town hated her and relocation was the only answer.

It was a small liberal town and I was one of the rare conservatives. I didn't like it/it made me sick.

In this era before computers it was important to be social but torture being around em all.

PEOPLE MADE ME SICK

Whether in church retreat, girl scout's camp in sixth grade or a sorority, people made me sick.

I felt insulted, questioned, perused, ridiculed. I couldn't wait to get home, I felt this all thru school.

People were always trying to get with me--impose on me--as I was trying to get away see.

Women were Jezebels behind my back, men were aggressively trying to get too close in fact.

The feeling of being imposed on/invaded increased with the years. Involvements brought tears.

Their interpersonal distance was much shorter [too close] and they stayed too long [get lost!].

That is the social culture: the herd, flock, school, tribe, clique, network or gang vs. the MATURE.

It's the individual vs. conformity to the social mazeway of that group: a transcender of the coop.

THE UNDERTOW

It happened a thousand times: the furtive glances and whisperings. I was so glad to be leaving.

Envision an area map with black paint splattered on it. Temporary blights in the social world are like it.

Fresh faces, innocent minds, positive welcomings, future optimism, happy smiles just by moving.

ANTI-FEMALE SPIRIT

It's the women having tantrums in police encounters. Not only daddy issues but attention whores.

It's scary when you think of it: how anti-female spirit they've become. Dull, husky and hardened.

When her queen spirit was broken she became fat and opaque: a used up darkened blank slate.

I see it with the polygamous ladies: some wear it well and some are broken and sink in their swill.

At this moment I am sovereign, fully protected and fenced. I don't intend to lose that assurance.

What's the most important thing in life to me? Not gold & silver, not homes & cars but a FENCE see.

There are many out there suffering [with people] like me but isolation has it's problems too see.

But as long as you know what's going on--hereby fully equipped--there will be no problem!

Letting ruffians in her home is the surest sign of female immaturity and sinful lusts too see.

A godly female would have more respect for her home and the others in it, to let in that element.

THE UNDERTOW

A sinful female has low self-esteem which demands approval-getting schemes from men it seems.

Let a man in your home and he aggresses, comes off too strong with in your face questions, yuk!

You may aggress on a woman in your home but not her in her home. But few have learned that son.

NO PRIVACY IN BEDLAM

But if a woman cannot enforce that posture they are compelled to bust her boundaries further.

Just listen to them: it's bedlam. Everyone chirping at the same time like kids going for attention.

Getting privacy in a social generation is a rare art form. It takes real muscle to stand up/not conform.

At a party there are two kinds of people: those who wanna leave and those who wanna stay until.

You can't calm her down or get her to shut up. Watch women in cop encounters: they go psychotic.

They assert dominance against the cop even knowing it'll get em arrested: it is that important.

They collapse into severe daddy issues, total immaturity and basically not knowing anything.

FURIOUS FEMALES

This is how they act in marriage. It's a round and round we go unmerry play of rage living in a cage.

Women are now ragaholics, compulsively fighting a false narrative bringing down their own house.

THE UNDERTOW

To be adversarial and competitive with their own husbands is the model and it stinks son.

When I got to a red area they were all into their own thing and no one was bugging me, happily.

Liberal sister pushed me to be social with a girl I didn't know. I find this ridiculous even now.

Fake smiles, hugs and virtue signaling. I can't stand it girl, don't pressure me to be part of it see.

Feminism has made women selfish, ego centered, foolish, fatuous and carnal/bloated.

There've been 85 million abortions since Roe vs Wade and that's as many depressions/suicides ok.

A woman who has had an abortion has "unexplained" rages towards her husband: hmmm....

To new wives: just perfect a few dishes he loves. Soon you'll have a week's rotation for the hus.

Bacon, beef, chicken, dairy, eggs and fish: this is what you stock up on/put in your freezer/fridge.

BREAKTHROUGH IS FROM GOD

Forget self-promotion. Let God promote you, let Him be your Champion. Besides, humility wins.

You don't need useless helpers. What you need is a BREAKTHROUGH and only God can do that sir.

All you can do in a dense generation is work then wait on God to light a match putting you first.

Your time will come: it has to happen when you're no longer hid under a bushel/God's thumb.

THE UNDERTOW

A Christian doesn't "update his social position" on modern issues, he's always the same Sue.

From Kindergarten I was afraid of my peers. Couldn't wait to go home & go deep inside/be a seer.

DONALD TRUMP AND POPULISM

All I know is how I felt when I heard him speak: Donald Trump brought reality and instant relief.

I knew every word was true, it's aesthetic knowledge we're born with and the opposite to liberals.

"Populism" is just common sense. We've had enough of self-appointed elites saying what's good for us.

These were not tweets put in books but points of a theory put daily on twitter to be understood.

So you're not a bible scholar—do you love the Lord? That's all that finally matters, I am sure.

The Bag Trick

PEOPLE AND CRUEL IMPRINTS
THE BAG TRICK
SEASON OF TREASON GANGUPS
HORRIBLE EXPERIENCES
KINGS TO PIGS: CALIBRATION
GO INNER ONLY
DON'T RECALL THE LOWER RUNGS
NEVER, EVER BE AN OPTION
BE ALONE UNTIL VALUED
LIBERAL KARMA
TRUST YOUR GUT ACHE
LIBERAL KARMA
LOSS OF IDENTITY AND TYRANNY
NEVER GET IN THEIR CAR
EFFECTS OF NARCISSISM
WE SHOULD WANT SOVEREIGNTY
THE TRUE VS FALSE SELF
PERSONALITY HIJACKING
LIBERAL KARMA

The Bag Trick

Hard times reveal true friends or cantankerous, jealous enemies coming with treachery.

Caving into little men tyrants who didn't even deserve a conversation with you: I was there too.

When choosing a mate find one who's SAFE. That's gotta be our new barometer I dare to say.

You can do something no one else can and you're about to be a millionaire from this talent man.

What you've been thru has been savage and cruel but you overcame it all and brilliantly came thru.

I'm proud of you tho' mom and dad isn't. We're a world force of rejects and the true God has risen.

You've taken people too seriously. They come and go but God is eternal, He's the Guy to know see.

PEOPLE AND CRUEL IMPRINTS

People are cruel and sometimes we end up hating God cuza that. Devastating lows: life goes flat.

I know what it's like being overlooked, shunned, ignored, falsely compared and discarded.

That's the herd: it leaves an inhumane imprint on us. You must separate, carve out your uniqueness.

People are cruel. They'll collude with your siblings against you if it pays well & degrades you too.

But things always even out in the end. Remember that now and things will start to turn around friend.

THE BAG TRICK

THE BAG TRICK

There's so many toxic recalls, put em ALL in a bag then throw the entire bag out. There's just too much.

If you were insane for a season you have thousands of such toxic recalls--throw the whole bag out.

To be as high as you are today you'd have to go that low ok, so to hang on thru PTSD is a time waste.

A season with those demons means many toxic recalls so the bag trick is whatcha call ESSENTIAL.

In the same way, stop recalling all THEY did. It's all an archetype evoked--the behaviors follow script.

Lord, what they put me thru! A generation without God or morals, brainwashed in public schools.

It was a land without justice nor lines. It was utter nonsensical emptiness and I was terrified.

SEASON OF TREASON GANGUPS

People ganged up on me too. They always will since they're herd animals mobbing up to be cruel.

Everyone was against me but it was principalities and powers along with a downed hedge see.

In my season of treason all were against me and I couldn't trust family/friends, like Job see.

It was a season, tho' a wretched one. But also the season of winning, favor and remuneration.

Every fairy tale, myth or story ending with winning starts with the canyon of evil or sinning.

HORRIBLE EXPERIENCES

THE BAG TRICK

The people I met/things I experienced were so horrible but in mental illness I gave my full acceptance.

The mental illness was: lack of boundaries allowing invasion without qualification, i.e. skuzz.

Let the past drop like a rock: THUD! Envision a big black boulder exploding on the ocean bot.

God can't do a new thing until we drop the old thing, the past. Can you let it go to have a blast?

It hurts as the past comes up and these experiences are revealed. Denial saved us then too.

The events coming up were so horrible I had to relive them to let them go. Pray: Help me God!

What put us in this fog? Conformity to false narratives, aetheism, media, hedonism, the social world.

You're swimming in the mud and can't see it cuz adaptation made it mundane/we even like it.

If you have God you have cornucopia, no dull bland grey roadmap of reality, the boring/unmiraculous.

KINGS TO PIGS: CALIBRATION

For there is a calibration to human nature high to low and you want the highest, don't you now?

Rejection did something to my soul and I became immature. It was regression/taking the lure.

With age she settles for less but she shouldn't do this for living with a lunatic--there's nothing worse.

I shoulda just gone into solitude and allowed the Potter to build me back up, not sink in my swill, yuk.

THE BAG TRICK

I was naive about old men too. Figuring them to be nice and kindly I got snagged bad in libel/lawsuits.

Young men must be trained how not to bust my boundaries constantly or bring their friends see.

GO INNER ONLY

You're too outward. Get more inner and God'll bring you out from obscurity/you'll be the winner.

You've done the work so just prepare for success. God planned both the beginning and the end sis.

Stop worrying and envision total renowned world success. To attract it you must HOLD to this.

Your wardrobe is perfect, you home too. Your diet is perfect and cookery too: you're ready Sue.

Don't pray for this or that but BREAKTHROUGH cuz God knows what you need, He's your Dad.

I don't need to define it to know that it exists: There's a natural calibration to humans, king to pigs.

DON'T RECALL THE LOWER RUNGS

Don't go back to what it's like on the lower rungs. It's an anchor to old soul ties and false friends.

If he treats you as just one among many then that's all you need to know honey: drop the phony.

A wicked messenger falls into trouble. He brings evil gossip from someone you didn't even know.

The more we appreciate what we have the more fulfilled we become. The problem: feeling lack.

THE BAG TRICK

Each day, hour and minute is different but all seems the same to someone stuck in the left brain.

The left brain is endless repetition of arguments too. Relationships are dull not vibrant and full.

The greatest truth is to exclude and not to add, so empty yourself completely then add back.

No one is too busy, it's just a matter of priorities. See that and be free of social anxieties.

Never force, don't beg and don't chase. I know it is easy to text/call a man but a woman shouldn't ok.

Don't worry your public faux paus. It's the devil but God said believers would not be condemned at all.

NEVER, EVER BE AN OPTION

If people treat you like an option, leave them like a choice and never look back [forget em].

Patience is your ally--why? Cuz everything falls into place if you just wait, and rushing is your enemy.

Despite what happened in the past you can always begin again no matter how much you sinned.

How to make it big: make yourself as small as you can. So humble you're lit as God is your Champion.

So you had to go thru the worst to get to the best. That's the way it works so forget the past.

God is your Champion, He'll know when the work is done and when/how to produce it for mon.

BE ALONE UNTIL VALUED

THE BAG TRICK

Be alone until you're valued. Unfair comparisons will bring you down, stay away from the herd Sue.

Hard times reveal true friends but even they will go away if you cling to crutches/addictions.

They're not smart enough to value you so hanging with them will make you feel misjudged and blue.

I had an ache in my gut all the time, a feeling of homesickness: my identity had been eclipsed.

I lost my identity to the wicked around me. By not being boundaried I'd been invaded spiritually.

I love my neighbor, a sweet little lady. But I'm boundaried and she knows it: I love freedom/privacy.

TRUST YOUR GUT ACHE

I had a gut ache in the false church, in the sorority, anywhere actually. Only solitude was friendly.

Extreme ectoverts prefer privacy, with the temperament of cerebrotonia, hating chaos see.

With privacy there is total control, around people there is none and you're an open wound to poke.

Then, when you've overcome all and are finally perfect, they pull the age card. That's the herd sir.

With every single toxic recall, envision the ROCK exploding on the bottom of the ocean, by God.

Years of therapy or just build boundaries? For the problem is a spiritual invasion of other entitles.

People treated you badly cuz it was your season of treason and the hedge was down: reason.

THE BAG TRICK

You anger God, the hedge of protection goes down. That's the key to avoid invasion of nation/home

Once safely in new surroundings the new events gradually replace old toxic memories.

LOSS OF IDENTITY AND TYRANNY

The more you know the dumber you sound to stupid people. The solution: be humble/avoid evil.

Stop comparing yourself to those starting decades after you. Live your own journey in lieu.

I nursed my extreme sense of isolation and alienation even in family with crutches. It was hell sis.

Until you build your own identity--on the Potter's wheel--you're liable to evil dependencies.

If not independent you're at the mercy of other people--and here there is no protection from evil.

Feeling my identity being annihilated frightened me, so I did everything to achieve it myself see.

I achieved while I isolated from involvements, having learned my lesson about about all of em.

I achieved while I isolated from involvements, having learned my fatal lesson about all of em.

NEVER GET IN THEIR CAR

For once you're in their car or once a man's in your house your destiny can change of course.

Homeless is horrible for loss of protection from the elements but MOSTLY from other people, amen.

THE BAG TRICK

I built identity thru achievement and expanded talents, to use them. And home, that's the main one.

They ask me to go off with them somewhere and I never will: never, ever be captive in an automobile.

You have evil helpers like some women. They get you in their car and start barking at you like vermin.

Tyranny takes over cuz they got control over you. They become totally different: note this lesson Sue.

Don't lose your independence cuz that is your identity. Losing sovereignty is self-treachery.

Lord, give us independence from prevalent people problems. Keep us safe in our homes, amen.

ALL bad decisions came either from people influence or negative emotions. Stay logical and win.

Prepare for your latter days which may resemble mysticism, infantilism or psychosis--so what.

EFFECTS OF NARCISSISM

Confusion, self-doubt, suicidation: these are the common outcomes of narcissistic abuse son.

Gotta know you're superior, there's no other way. Otherwise you're familiar and they bash ok.

One may smile, and smile, and be a villain. We gotta see thru masks and smirks makes me question.

God's in control over all evil things if you don't get involved with the world, like having flings.

No one is as single as a married narcissist. They flirt, they eye the new supply, they don't resist.

THE BAG TRICK

I just wanna stay home! I love the pleasures, seasons, routines and comforts therein, never to roam.

I'm not interested in traveling or going to conventions. Don't bore me with the traditions of men.

The only thing I control is my home so that's where I stay, free of freakish accidents or mistakes.

WE SHOULD WANT SOVEREIGNTY

I worked all my life for my own home--i.e. sovereignty--where I could be free of human tyranny.

We must be stoic at the fleetiness of life/inevitability of setbacks, having stability amidst chaos.

The folly of fools is deceiving. The good man is clearly discerned but the virtue signaling is a stink.

In toil there is profit but mere talk leads to poverty. Sick of trying to adapt socially? Choose prosperity.

Don't dumb down just cuz they don't know what you're talking about. The answer is to remain stoic.

Avoiding evil is a fountain of life that one may turn away and avoid the snares of death. Proverbs

Hating white people is not considered racist to the left. It's just another way they gotcha, but resist.

Biden's prospective one world communist melting pot is a case of paradise lost but it's all we got.

They're culture-vultures: going along with woke garbage just to get elected or hired.

It's not that you want to be famous but there are mass attractions to the true self once finished.

THE BAG TRICK

THE TRUE VS FALSE SELF

Self-control is a fruit of the spirit so if you don't have it I gotta wonder about you but I'll hide it.

The false self is horrible. It does things to be noticed and in the long run will never be trusted.

Can't know what a narcissist is til you've been abused. The discard's enough to feel eternally screwed.

To be lovebombed then dropped is enough to change consciousness for life, feeling like a flop.

To be lovebombed then dropped is enough to change consciousness for life, feeling like a flop.

I can't follow all your words and don't intend to try. Learn to be terse and laconic, that's high.

They need fossils so why mask age or try to relate? Give what you have from years overcoming hate.

See competition as a good thing. Even insults create needed resistance to build queens/kings.

Here we think they're all talking about us when really we're just a grain a sand, no one gives a dam.

Without prayer we become a target for the enemy's counterfeit. Stay close to God to avoid it.

They disconnect you from your intuition by proving you can't trust your own logic or True Self son.

Having been vibrant, now you're blind in the dark bumping up against things and defiant.

PERSONALITY HIJACKING

THE BAG TRICK

You've been eclipsed by another human being, your personality highjacked and replaced see.

He sees women as goddesses or doormats and increasingly you're stepped on like that.

A sister could bully one until self-esteem is so run into the ground she loses reality/just gets drunk.

She may fly into the arms of another to get her identity back, as narc abuse causes ontological panic.

In a child it causes emotional dysregulation and eating disorders: using food to regulate emotion.

The maladaptive energy "lands" on an area like food or sex and grows into a self-protective colony.

The maladaptive coping device becomes an addiction protected by anosognosia/denial of problem.

Intentionally retrieve your True Self by sorting the true from the false introjections of the narcissist.

Find the loving, curious, adventurous cute kids you were before being tortured by the mockers.

Find the loving, curious, adventurous, cute kid you were before being tortured by the mockers.

LIBERAL KARMA

Liberal karma NYC: the architects are never the victims of their own policies but now they will be.

They moved us to be a globalist multicultural atomized hodgepot and well hell, we all hate it a lot.

How could one stupid broad lead the squad which led the democrats into this destructive fraud?

MORAL MADNESS

MORAL MADNESS

MORAL INJURY

PTSD or moral injury? Did you witness events so intolerable that it ruined your personality?

Moral injury brings the opposite personality. Lines, boundaries, theories are all reversed see.

We swim in muddy waters as our conscience is seared and we go against all we know/Godly fear.

Acting against one's own conscience is a serious rift so social psychology becomes a moral psychiatry.

Moral madness [moral insanity] is acting the opposite to the true self in every realm or intensity.

Decades after repentance one is still sorting out the confusion so keep it simple: it was the devil.

I didn't believe in anything I was doing but social approval was more important to me.

I suffered so much with boredom I ended up going solo anyway, the only path making sense to me.

A moral elitist, that's a happy carefree life which is freest taking guts, strength and boldness.

If you don't firmly draw and maintain boundaries the evil world flows in like a killer tsunami.

The evil intruder always brings his friends and other jokers and out of pure fear you take the lure.

MORAL MADNESS

MORAL MADNESS

You sense violence in your bones and every thought: PTSD for accepting what you shoulda fought.

Were you morally mad for an era? Did this sequence follow trauma? That's how it works sista.

See moral madness is the OPPOSITE to the true self in every realm and you'll understand the harm.

If behavior's opposed to the True Self's truth, it's also irrational, bizarre and mistake driven too.

It's not an insane person just traumatized into moral madness in an era, tho' shocking to friends.

Losing all judgment and moral compass for an era, a result of trauma: is this not modern America?

Moral madness is a period of great pride mixed with bitter resentment and morbid shame, aye.

Going against all you know puts the body thru the ringer as everything's reversed/from high to low.

Guilt, shame and remorse must be covered up and now you have another blind area of anosognosia.

WEAKNESS BRINGS IMMORALITY

A woman gives in sexually rather than be called silly and pays for it with a life of morbid memories.

Don't let a man touch you, don't get in his car and don't let him in: eternal advice to all generations.

Weakness is an entry point to demons who instruct the personality how to behave in evil ways.

NONE of that was me for I'm a sweet little lady. It was an introject from trauma but now I'm free ok.

MORAL MADNESS

TRAUMA AND DISTORTED IMPLANTS

Trauma is how moral madness is passed on to new generations, it's truly the initiation rite son.

Trauma also creates AUTONOMISMS, uncontrollable uprushes from the unconscious that are alien.

Don't deflate from remorse, you weren't yourself. This was ego-alien material while you're a kind elf.

Just be the cute little elf again and relocate if you can cuz they won't let you up sometimes man.

Find the loving, curious, adventurous, cute kid you were before being tortured by mockers.

It all starts with the narcissist, believe me--as he intervened between you and true reality.

Not only do they impose their reality, they intimidate constantly and most like me cave in see.

When your own true vibrant personality is eclipsed by a parasite sponger, life is dim and very scary.

Making gold, or the transmutation of energy, is a time of sorting the true from the false and simplicity.

Unpeeling distorted implants from those long dead and for heaven's sake starting all over again fresh.

SCAPEGOAT IS THE EMPATH

The scapegoat target is the empath who receives a big boulder from the bloodline: I was that Lass.

The chosen target is the one revealing the image magic of the sick system and her life will be tragic.

MORAL MADNESS

The chosen target is the one revealing the sick system's image magic, so her life could be hard/tragic.

Season of treason is filled with mental illness and stupid cruelty so throw out the bag sweetie.

Throw out the whole bag: the years of humiliation and counter responses that all held you back.

Those with BIG personalities muffled really suffer as life goes by in a blur and their plans are troubled.

Expurgate dusty/distorted implants, refind the true self and dust off your plans. Go ahead now man.

The most energetic become the most tragic as that energy drives inward to self-destructive sick.

ECLIPSED BY PARASITE SPONGERS

When your true vibrant personality is eclipsed by a parasite sponger, life goes dim/happy no longer.

Can't change what they said about you when down. Hot coals on their head now you're renowned.

It's a female demon fueled by alcohol. That was mom's influence taking years getting free of it all.

The minute she gets an upper hand she goes tyrant. Harridans are weak, that's how you tell it.

Your persecutors are gone but still in your head, making you crazy with what you shoulda said.

Your mockers are sick, old, jailed, toothless or dead but you're still sore how they treated you then.

By agreeing with them/denying who I was, I lost personal reality and walked around in a fuzz.

MORAL MADNESS

When we take on the reality of others about ourselves or them it's THE END but it's very common.

Activate the flow by turning all your attention on a loving God by praying "as above, so below".

Don't drain your latter days with bad memories. Put the past in a bag/God puts to bottom of the sea.

Satan pops bad memories into your mind. At that time think "put it all in a bag and throw to the wind."

You must look FORWARD in your latter days, not back. For it's never better the bible says in fact.

ADAPTATION TO IDIOTS
The Dunning-Kruger Effect

What I went thru was pure hell but worth it all to write to you guys about what it's like being unwell.

Tho' I was MADE unwell, I was too weak to resist tyranny and the distorted implants from hell.

You must be strong enough to maintain your reality in the face of enforced conformity to insanity.

As a woman I found their expectations, perceptions or projections onto me revolting and insulting.

Who the hell did they think they were? My spirit would rebel and that alone brought persecutors.

They knew nothing about me, my education or letters. So I got a taste of the expectations of losers.

It was a painful experiment in the Dunning-Kruger effect of having to adapt to idiots in fact.

The higher you are the less they can SEE who you are and to get outa this you gotta be really clever.

MORAL MADNESS

They always make you insecure and question yourself. They doubt your calibre and mental health.

Nothing's wrong but the alert system of your mind. Living in the past and wasting your time.

Be future oriented & drop the past like a rock. You don't have time, you've gotta destiny Dr. Kellock.

Refugees of war must go forward, for to relive the horrors brings aging/death like no tomorrow.

Stop recalling past bad actors put there to be your instructors. You have boundaries now/protectors.

LONELY RECLUSE ECCENTRIC

In that era I was intensely lonely but when people would come I was very unhappy/felt crazy.

Friends taught you what you could be, enemies what you must do: better put up firm boundaries.

Friends taught you what you could be, enemies what you must do: put up firm boundaries Sue.

It's hard realizing no one cares, but soon a light inside explodes with glee as God says "but I love thee".

No one gives a dam but I'm bitchen. No one gives a dam but I'm bitchen: My 16 year old chant.

TREACHEROUS OLD HARRIDANS

Since I didn't learn it from mom I had to learn it from a buncha mean and treacherous old harridans.

The minute you show weakness the bully bitches will tear you apart. I learned that from the start.

MORAL MADNESS

Before forgiving them it's like you're a slave to them. Disconnect by forgiving then forgetting em.

The path to the True Self is circuitous, zigzag, unpredictable and unplanned so just rest.

It may be you're supposed to dream all day if that's most productive you see, and its all ok.

THE NARC'S HENCHMEN

Not only do they wreak havoc in your life, they bring others equally entitled and filled with strife.

The narc involves you with other narcs: his henchmen are also cruel and cold, unempathic jerks.

Watch involvements for they spread out in concentric circles of evil, an intricate controlling labyrinth.

Watch who you marry cuz at low points you may be controlled by an evil member God didn't anoint.

You meet someone and suddenly all their friends and family. Don't get swept up, stay strong honey.

The marriage goes sour and now your fighting his kids who are no longer restrained by family ethics.

Watch your involvements because they're sticky [controlling] yet like sandpaper [grating].

STRANGER IN A STRANGE LAND

I felt like a stranger in a strange land. The discard made me mentally ill, no longer able to function man.

I didn't know and felt discordance with these people, my "family". That was fantasy, this was scary.

MORAL MADNESS

I felt like a stranger in a strange land. The discard made me mentally ill, not able to function again.

A conservative ostracized by an entire family of liberals: it was easy to slip back and give up all goals.

He presented himself as a caring, even weak person. They all start out that way so get a grip hon'.

TERRIFIED OF THE THRONGS

To do justice and judgement is more acceptable to the Lord than sacrifice. Proverbs 21: 3.

I will never beg and I'm number one or forget it so that narrows things down just to where I like it.

Those people made me terrified and disgusted. I only wanted to escape so took a drink/got busted.

Chemical sensitivities made terror worse which made the implications more profound, what a curse.

I was so utterly happy alone. Then suddenly I'm swept up into an army against me in my own home.

It was people who made me sick, sicker and sickest. When alone I'm a happy child every minute.

My high life is having a husband who gives me solitude and protects me from the other room.

With age I'm more self-protective. We see evil & hide from it--that's wisdom of the elect isn't it?

Once hooked into him and his group, he feeds them lies so they turn against you and you feel the fool.

When alone my reality was rich and colorful but when with others it became anxious, grey, awful.

MORAL MADNESS

First he says you're too cocky then too whiney then too clingy then too demanding and cranky see.

Happy home: health & beauty. Hostile environment: every known malady & saying to hell with it.

ATTEMPTED ESCAPES

First I escaped into movies then they became too much to track. There was too much inside in fact.

Normally the survival is activated then we go back into rest but this was constant, my skin was a mess.

It was like living in a communist country that way. A sense of intimidation or feeling afraid to say.

In a state of uncertainty rhythms are altered from your normalcy and other systems collapse quickly.

You are now in sympathetic dominance where fight, flight or fawn is activated all the time/at once.

THE JUNGLE MENTALITY

It's the jungle mentality of threat perception & stress responses that wreck the skin of the princess.

It's called walking on eggs/broken glass and I recall it well, I was sick as hell being that distressed.

I had to learn that I could never drink. To do that it was years up and down, ruined by being a fink.

With stress the gut shuts down to use energy for surviving and skin reflects the same thing.

The most important thing for health & beauty is a happy environment and every ethologist knows that.

MORAL MADNESS

Happy environment: predictable, growth-producing, creative, hospitable, sensual and pleasant.

You want him to become who he was not what he is--unrecognizable--so accept breadcrumbs.

Rather than seeing a child who needs to be cherished it's a nuisance groomed to comply and bashed.

They're arrogant but don't know much. Arrogance and ignorance is a terrible combination as such.

In high end neighborhoods you constantly hear the buzz of worker's tools as neighbors upgrade.

PROGRESSIVE POLICY

It's a top-down elite revolution, not a grass roots one. Open borders etc--all of it is hated by us son.

Climate emergency: something that isn't real but they do great damage on the basis of it see.

The worse policy is "temporary protected status" leading to a permanent magnet: MASSIVE.

Regulation is always creeping totalitarianism, whether it's about podcasts in Canada or our guns.

Regulation is when the home visiting bureaucrat rules, making you walk the plank like a dam fool.

The democrat party is the party of the confederacy, slavery and anti-Americanism. Mark Levin

The democrats trash the declaration of independence, the constitution and our economic system.

We no longer have a free press, just a press that's free to lie to us without any consequences.

MORAL MADNESS

It's a constant attack on the status quo of the existing society. There is a barrage of it in universities.

THE END RESULTS

10,000 days were bliss and only 10 days were trauma and stress. Why have PTSD over the latter sis?

Ok, so the old days are gone. But so are all your persecutors, and being on the lower rung.

Ten years in expanded consciousness becomes thirty, while ten being dense goes by in a blur/quickly.

Don't overshare because privacy is power. Stay a mystery and respect grows much further.

Christianity does not rest on mysticism or spiritual devices, e..g. magic healings like TV entices.

People come and go, they're not that important. It's God Who's eternally present but also the serpent.

God packs in the latter days. The past was a blur for decades but now it's fat cuz you're amazed.

I'm very happy in my home, having relocated to a safe place with a high wall and a locked gate.

I give him $100 and then never see him again. That's called the "promotion of your book" scam.

BUTTERED POPCORN IS KETO

Gut and brain health are linked. Does this mean we get IBS because we are depressed, you think?

Popcorn is keto and butter is zero so have at it: all the buttered popcorn you want, for glow.

ERA OF NIGHTMARES

TWO [OPPOSITE] PEOPLE IN ONE
CRUEL SEXUAL MARKET VALUE
WE SWIM IN MUDDY WATERS
INFERIOR MAN IS A SUCK-UP JERK
WAKING UP TO A BLOODY NIGHTMARE
REP-DESTROYING SISTERS
TRUE EXPERIENCE IS OUR SCHOOL
SUCCESS: GIFTS & PASSION
LYING AND STATUS QUO GUARDING
THEY CONDEMN THE RIGHTEOUS
HIT MEN [FLYING MONKEYS]
HYPER-CARNIVORE
I VOTE FOR STIR FRY
BLATANT ANTISEMITISM REVEALED
DEATH OF THE PROGRESSIVE MOVEMENT
CALLOUS STUDENTS HEX
NOTES FOR CHAMPS AND SUCCESS

ERA OF NIGHTMARES

TWO [OPPOSITE] PEOPLE IN ONE

It's not masculinity when he's asking you for money. He's just a weasel lady, get a new steady.

Never move in with a man lest he takes his name off the deed and puts yours on. It's too dangerous hon'.

Everyone has two sides and he could change--and it's the nicest guys who become the worst ok.

Stay grounded, for the "nicest of all women" become the worst when their nicey image lets down.

There are two separate nervous systems & two sides to the brain: two opposite people in one ok.

At least with a terrorist you know he's evil, not with the mixed signals & subterfuges of normal people.

The love of God is the hatred of evil. It's not only men who go to war, we gotta purge it out too.

You're a daughter of the most high God, not someone with low SMV because of your age [fraud].

CRUEL SEXUAL MARKET VALUE

SMV: Sexual Market Value is a cruel concept of perverted male society making it true see.

"I don't want her, you can have her, she's too fat/old for me." The callous atmosphere of treachery.

ERA OF NIGHTMARES

If you let monsters outa the cage they'll eat the sheep. That means: don't let them in, the creeps.

WE SWIM IN MUDDY WATERS

We swim in muddy waters so repent and it's over. God forgets it too so just don't repeat the error.

Since 99.99% of your problems were self-generated, you can finally relax now you've repented.

A lady has firm boundaries. She is not lax/easy for to suffer invasion is degrading to queens/ladies.

If creative they treat you like an oddball but if you've made it they don't treat you like that at all.

It's called a "dogmatic deflection" when they doggedly avoid all facts and rational conversation.

INFERIOR MAN IS A SUCK-UP JERK

Inferior man is two pronged: a suckup to supposed superiors and a real jerk to those below him.

A sick system is like being in a cage. You're the recipient--can't get away--from all their rage.

Friends are discouraged when one refuses to condemn evil and even takes it back repeatedly too.

He destroyed my dreams and unleashed a nightmare. My esteem collapsed down and I didn't care.

I came from dysfunction then went to a woke college. Then came mental illness called privilege.

WAKING UP TO A BLOODY NIGHTMARE

ERA OF NIGHTMARES

It was like waking up to a bloody nightmare I didn't see at the time tho' my body suffered greatly, aye.

Risk your life for the cause of freedom and all you get is dehumanized and villainized, under the gun.

10,000 days were great but five days were bad. Yet the latter gave her PTSD and she ended in bed.

10,000 days bliss, 5 days social trauma. You'd think the latter would disappear but it stays with ya.

When your own sibling is the worst persecutor of your soul: sister abuse is a real thing you know.

REP-DESTROYING SISTERS

When your own sister destroys your rep like none other: sibling abuse is a real thing and never over.

She was all for Pocahontas [Warren] and Bernie the communist but thought she knew the most.

Who else does she have to abuse? What women are like when they get the power to confuse.

Way to stay out of trouble and have a peaceful life: avoid the people and things causing strife.

It's not blaming others to realize 99% of your trouble coulda been avoided by blocking those guys.

The only problem in you was weak boundaries not something inherent in yourself see.

Ukraine: the biggest money laundering scheme in history, all going back to democrat pockets see.

TRUE EXPERIENCE IS OUR SCHOOL

ERA OF NIGHTMARES

Maturity is avoidance while immaturity is letting em all in and being degraded 'til you collapse.

Reading about the storm isn't the same as weathering one. Experience is gold, bookishness is none.

It's in the heart of the storm and gusty wind that real lessons are learned: the inoculation of hurt.

Gifts plus passion is what brings success. It was your experience that brings this combination sis.

Systems theory formed the basis in school but hurtful relationships were the real educative tool.

Never bemoan the lost years, those were your Ph.D. in the Streets which gave you character dear.

SUCCESS: GIFTS & PASSION

Gifts plus passion is what brings success. It's your experiences that trigger this combination sis.

Every bad, sordid, painful or perverted relationship could bring wisdom and purity in rebellion.

Overcoming these obstacles brought character and this will be written on your face in the future.

My level of disgust was so intense I had to build a high fence and I've been euphoric ever since.

The more disgust the higher the fence. I had to go thru hell to acquire boundaries for self-defense.

It doesn't matter we're a speck of sand, God still puts us first cuz omniscience is His attribute man.

Isn't looking young, looking healthy? It's ageless, but then if you eat crap you'll look your age see.

ERA OF NIGHTMARES

For success melt passion with talents. It's your deep emotion bringing you passion so go for it.

LYING AND STATUS QUO GUARDING

Lying goes with status quo guarding. With deception it's so precarious they won't try a thing.

Pain is a learning experience, it helps you find strength. You rely more on God for life, the full length.

I'm very considerate or at least I'm told that. But I'm not a coddler and will surely call them out on it.

The new age is all about "bothsides-ism". They always say both are a problem, hiding truth son.

It's a great relief to realize the work has already been done. Now enjoy the fruits of your labor/fun.

It's a great relief to see the work has already been done. Now enjoy the fruits of your labor/have fun.

Beware of evil helpers. They worm their way in then gossip to the streets about all your blunders.

THEY CONDEMN THE RIGHTEOUS

It's an abomination to condemn the righteous while justifying the wicked but the liberals did it.

No worries, when your views prove to be true people's attitude towards you change dramatically too.

He who loves transgression loves strife. It's so nice to have peace in your home, that's the high life.

Recalcitrant, sarcastic teens: bat them down. For the most important thing is PEACE in your home.

ERA OF NIGHTMARES

Strife is a demon sent from hell. Angry words, even nonverbal slurs: nip em in the bud, farewell.

Unfair comparisons: that's violence too. You can feel it in your soul and that's all you need Sue.

HIT MEN [FLYING MONKEYS]

She never hit me, she'd incite others to or create a scene. She was equally guilty the law decrees.

He saves you from troubles only to put you back in his bubble. Ask God, He pays ya back double.

Those with a seared conscience show utter callousness. It just makes ya sick to witness it.

The minute he got in my home he took over. You can't take a chance, let no one in here sister.

It wasn't people, it was evil principalities/powers coming through in your season of being screwed.

They can't see evil tho' it's staring them in the face. These are virtue signalers, what a disgrace.

While being "always happy" they miss that dangerous moment when they should be prepared/ready.

University support for Hamas proves the moral & intellectual rot in higher education does it not?

HYPER-CARNIVORE

Carnivore is meat only [LEG CRAMPS]. Hyper-carnivore is raw dairy and fruit 30% with meat 70%.

In his car it was like a wall hit me chemically and I was never the same after that chemical injury.

ERA OF NIGHTMARES

Most plants don't wanna be eaten but the fruits do so the seeds are spread through defecation.

The self-defense mechanisms in plants [veggies] bring IBS, GERD, acid reflux, constipation etc. see.

If you can stand the chance of extreme muscle cramps, then try going all meat with no fruit or plants.

100% meat is not for me as I fear going to sleep and waking up with another Charlie Horse see.

The charlie horses got so bad I feared I'd be in a wheelchair soon or that I had M.S., doom.

Hyper-carnivore is for people like me with extreme sensitivity: get protein punch without disability.

It really is about portion control. I can eat popcorn once but if I eat it twice I have trouble at night.

Stir fry: fry up your meat, put it away. Fry the cut veggies now add the meat, spices and sauce ok.

I VOTE FOR STIR FRY

Stir fry is always fresh, delicious, quick and easy. Just buy thin sliced beef etc., it all ends perfectly.

Chuck roast is how you get pull-apart beef. It's also easy to eat and it goes with all ethnicities.

Ginger and garlic: great for my poor stomach. Mongolian beef, pepper steak, how I love it.

When we have bacon and eggs for breakfast, that's it for a day. So satiating, so cheap in that way.

Freezer meals: chicken parmasan, beef chili, chicken cacciatore, steak stroganoff—made on day off.

ERA OF NIGHTMARES

BLATANT ANTISEMITISM REVEALED

The newly revealed and blatant antisemitism of the left is the last straw, the turning point in thought.

"The antisemitic spirit of World War II will never happen again". Nip this in the bud or it will my friend.

Biden shows desperation establishing communication with those wanting to kill us and him.

Low IQ problems: anger, depression, bipolarity, aggression. Not a productive population.

They're bred to be evil and stupid but we're the bad ones cuz we wanna fight back? Forget it.

All it shows is the democrats have lost the ability to hate evil. They have no sympathy for people.

If they don't even treat their own citizens humanely why would they care about the hostages see.

Goodness says: "they're all animals" while evil says "they're all God's children". What a separation.

DEATH OF THE PROGRESSIVE MOVEMENT

Progressive movement in it's death throes: So many thought it meant they were good fellows.

I will not hate you for killing my children, but for making me kill your children. Golda Meir

Mormon neighborhoods are peaceful. They don't drink and are well armed, keeping things tranquil.

The fact nothing has happened with the mass border crossings indicates sleeper cells waiting.

ERA OF NIGHTMARES

If you disagree with the group that much you gotta denounce the group and announce that too.

To root out evil unfortunately you have to kill a lot of people. That's a reality learned from WWII.

Hiroshima, Nagasaki, leveled German cities: masses of innocents killed to root out aggressors/Nazis.

Many middle eastern nations were getting along and doing business with Israel, save these few.

CALLOUS STUDENTS HEX

Students callously disregard this barbaric torture since they're already seared as an abortion culture.

Those who are compassionate to the cruel will end up being cruel to the compassionate too.

We can't tolerate barbarity being ignored for we can't chance it happening again going forward.

The love of God and wisdom itself is the hatred of evil. Don't go easy just cuz others told you to.

Big difference between deliberate targeting of civilians and inevitable deaths from the fog of war then.

Liberals brought a buncha strangers to my house. Similarly, their border's open to any louse.

It's not just killing but horrific killing in the spirit of Jihad, a principality of demons opposing God.

NOTES FOR CHAMPS AND SUCCESS

All you gotta do for success is tell the world WHY your way is better--and nothing could be easier.

ERA OF NIGHTMARES

Never write until prompted. The gem must well up coming THRU you, writing it down promptly.

Why would they rock the boat by letting you in? You're too truthtelling and independent, hating sin.

There's an evil army all around and it hates how you're so profound. Stay alone, work until summoned.

You've laid a helluva seed. Now like a good farmer you WAIT, of course not expecting it immediately.

A crooked heart can't discover. You can't be a discoverer in art, science, literature unless pure.

The herd sees aging as subtraction--not addition--but it means superior completion of the person.

They're on the horn all day ruining reputations. That's how women rule their domain from home.

Their evil is so bad you can't deal with it. Now turn your back and never look back, or forget it.

QUEENDUMB

GET PAST PEOPLE
QUEEN OR DUMB
LET SELF-RESPECT ERECT
TWISTED NEED FOR ACCEPTANCE
BE NOT CONFORMED TO THE WORLD
LOOK AT IT BIOLOGICALLY
BEGGING FOR CONSIDERATION
SOLITUDE THRU BOUNDARIES
SECLUSION ATTRACTS FAME
YOUR LESSONS WERE HARD
DESTINY IS WITH GOD NOT MAN
THEY WANT SOMETHING
LETTING THE BOYS IN
NO CHANCE OF LOOKING BAD
DON'T LET EM IN/GO TO THE DOOR
WEASELLY

QUEENDUMB

First he came to visit me and I let him in. Then he asked to do his laundry and then for money again.

GET PAST PEOPLE

Managed solitude in a safe place: that's the greatest accomplishment of anyone in our present age.

Your reward is solitude bliss by not having those people around anymore, as your spirit will soar.

You reward: getting your life back, every inch and minute bringing order where there was lack.

You will realize with time and even decades later how they sapped your spirit [almost] forever.

You won't believe the things you put up with, blinded by your need for approval from rubbish.

New location, new public image. Because it's all social psychology via gossip determining it.

QUEEN OR DUMB

A queen is never rejected but if she is she walks away gently and never again thinks of the enemy.

After he rejects, he's shit. Dust off your hands and wish em well but don't lurk anymore just split.

QUEENDUMB

I couldn't believe how people treated me. I got a slice of how it felt to be a Jew in Nazi Germany.

I don't want my thoughts to cloud with you anymore. Therefore I won't allow them to go there.

Dust off your hands and get the hell away gently: always have class about it but get on quickly,

Now don't think another thing about it, he chose someone else but you've escaped a noose.

LET SELF-RESPECT ERECT

Let these words sink in and stop your lurking. You're above all this and it's just plain degrading.

He may as well be in the room so get some self-control girl or be mentally/emotionally screwed.

Don't allow your mind to go there for it's a battlefield between good and evil: check your people.

Don't worry about the enemy. People get heady, make mistakes and bring the ship down surely.

Be gentle to yourself, that's number one. Stop lurking outa curiosity which kills the cat/no fun.

Don't give them ANY ENERGY, hear me? You should be dusting off your hands, not lurking!

He treated you like a pig or a Jew in Nazi Germany and you give him your thoughts? Be free!

TWISTED NEED FOR ACCEPTANCE

Her thinking's broken by a perverted generation of men twisting her need for acceptance from them.

QUEENDUMB

We have an innate need for male acceptance and they've used that to bash our confidence.

She desires acceptance of men beneath her when she doesn't know who she is, a budding star.

Sick relationships allowed to endure extend brokenness until a queen rises from the mess.

They control by breaking her self-esteem: of being sovereign and happy like a queen.

When her mindset changes the movement of her life changes into success as her God arranges.

Be not conformed to this world but be transformed by the renewal of your mind: from low to high.

There's a world system designed to cave in, miniaturize, squeeze and shrink you and it hurts Sue.

BE NOT CONFORMED TO THE WORLD

Be not conformed--made smaller than you are--but be transformed: become BIGGER, like a star.

In breaking from that system you transform to what God pre-designed for you, His man/woman.

Refusing to conform was a hard rode esp. for a female. They all rose up against me/wanted me to fail.

But I wasn't going to be treated like that, with such disdain and superiority. I was queenly see.

Seeking approval of some undeserving man and never seeking God, the Key to freedom in the land.

Men acting like they owned me: wicked bands of possession I felt all through life even as a teen.

QUEENDUMB

Men shit-testing or traumatizing me to put me in my place: Being a jerk was how they ruled ok.

I became afraid to be alone with them. I felt anxiety until I learned to put boundaries down.

This justified anxiety is why "women should never have men in their home when alone" I guess see.

They take over aggressively when immature, they move in calmly, slowly and surely when mature.

Meet with men when chaperoned and never alone. This has saved me so much trouble I see around.

LOOK AT IT BIOLOGICALLY

Look at it biologically: would you allow a bigger animal in your cage? To be trapped all day afraid?

Marriage is a fence: coming behind a wall protecting from this undertow, a self-esteem defense.

We should want the approval of our Creator but if it's for men we're steered down to the gutter.

A system establishes mindset from the outside world and no one builds the self-esteem of the girl.

Growing up with broken mindset needing the affirmation of significant male who may reject.

When a young boy detects her need for affirmation he demands she perform for it: here it began.

"I'm a boss chick" but she has petty jealousies within her circle: on the phone she controls it all.

A true king is never intimidated by woman so he doesn't have to constantly break her down, amen?

QUEENDUMB

Some are so desperate to be wives they settle for stuff that is less than a husband, even strife.

Relational choices: the greatest reflection of mindset, and the bad ones continue to deteriorate it.

Until her mindset changes she'll continue to mindlessly let em in or when they ask be a yes person.

I was such a wimp I'd lie: "my family is coming so you gotta leave" rather than "I'm busy, leave please."

It was always "my family is here" to get out of things, never standing up for my own solitude see.

BEGGING FOR CONSIDERATION

I had to beg for any consideration for me: a black and white difference from my present jubilee.

When he came to the door I'd run and hide rather than just telling him to scram for good, aye.

It took years to recognize my anxiety around people and to prefer solitude in the home, free of evil.

They were jealous of my comfortable surroundings and wanted to come and live with me always.

I couldn't get rid of em and when I finally forced a break they'd retaliate like as if it was an amputate.

These were lost and lonely souls from dysfunctional homes with no father and feminist moms.

As I progressed as writer I couldn't tolerate casual drop-ins and had to FIGHT for aloneness.

It was a FIGHT to win solitude. It was a reward after a decades war with Jezebel spirits and dudes.

QUEENDUMB

With a pure and high archetype there are mass attractions to the true self and we need a wall.

You can't train a narcissist to abide your boundaries. You want a formal lifestyle now for ladies.

SOLITUDE THRU BOUNDARIES

Once I saw to protect myself all these people problems ended: I could spread my wings as gifted.

He's disrespectful and does nothing to advance your life. He's either in your bed or causing strife.

Lay a boundary, the narcissist busts it. You can't take him up with you, elites can't accept this.

You're FREE when you're retired from society. It's a shame we can't be wise when young, truly.

A queen needs more than sex, she needs a man with character, vision, backbone, standards.

I've got to have a man with spirituality who can LEAD ME: that's what every woman wants see.

It's cool when we go thru things and no one can tell because we remain the same. Joyce Meyer

For people are so empty in this social era that any realized person is a magnet to em, I swear.

Take a chance to really think about this before we proceed. That's how important it is to secede.

SECLUSION ATTRACTS FAME

It's a paradox: go into seclusion, find the treasure hard to attain—the true self, expect mass attractions.

QUEENDUMB

Desire social approval, fail miserably. Want solitude, they can't get enough and attract in see.

It's a paradox: go into seclusion, find the self/treasure hard to obtain and mass attractions attain.

Narcissists wanna ignore what started it too, saying "let's go forward" tho' you were screwed.

The petty jealous young women love to bash the elder but the harridans get back at them later.

To the elders: never get stuck competing with youth for it's a yelling game and humiliating too.

Queen conscious women don't date randomly for to let him in is a big deal/dangerous potentially.

The queen dates intentionally, for the purpose of gathering data on this guy re: marriage.

You never yoke a donkey with a horse. Different strengths/temperaments make it hard.

YOUR LESSONS WERE HARD

Your lessons were hard/thorny. People problems are excruciating but it's the price of wisdom see.

Two animals are yoked for the purpose of productivity and this is the way marriage should be.

You got too involved too quick and that's the reason it failed and you suffered for decades hick.

You gave that man privileges of a husband and right away you weren't/will never be the virtuous one.

You gave him your life story too quick. You're just gathering data not being a little girl or a hick.

QUEENDUMB

Be proud of yourself, you've come so far. But the system capped your self-esteem, your star.

They don't want no queen consclousness, they want you subservient and conforming sis.

How much more for the purpose of productivity when one ties his life to another for eternity?

I want neighbors who are nice to me, ready to help me in emergency but otherwise give me privacy.

DESTINY IS WITH GOD NOT MAN

Our identity is not tied up with a man but with the Creator, how HE sees us and our behavior.

Not knowing self is why you choose people who break you down--water seeks its own level hon'.

A breakup is an opportunity to come to self--the most rewarding, exhilarating trip on earth.

You've got talents eclipsed by this guy. You lost contact with destiny written in your DNA/the sky.

You gotta know who you are and where you're going or dating ends in pain [it's disappointing].

Never invest in a man's business ideas. This is the biggest game running so ignore this phony.

I attracted alot of this. It reminded me of the eighties when they'd come to me for drug money.

THEY WANT SOMETHING

He wants something from you, all for your own good! Don't bat an eyelash, reject this hick/hood.

QUEENDUMB

Any man wanting YOU to invest in HIS dream is suspect. See this & don't be swayed by sex.

He's looking at you as nothing but a check. Sure he'll have sex cuz he wants that too you hick.

He'll strong-arm/hypnotize you thru sex to invest in his business ideas! Always recall these words sis!

They saw me as successful and wanted to get some of it, hopeful. This was a new level/new devil.

A good man with character to sustain you will never risk giving you the impression he's using you.

I'm very generous, ask anyone in my circle. But this thing about winey/weasel men is trouble.

When young all trauma-based energy landed on food and booze. Now I'm sober/letting pot go too.

I was so severely traumatized I just sought crutches, the only way I could tolerate life in the ditches.

LETTING THE BOYS IN

Due to diverse lusts and laden with sins, I let the boys in and didn't even know any better it seems.

It was horrible what they put me thru, I had no idea people acted like this! Naivete, innocence.

Being cerebrotonic with fear of disorder, this sudden bedlam in my home shocked me forever.

Being adaptive, this shock was transmuted to a rod of iron about privacy from then on: reclusive.

The new age said people were good and we were neurotic for fearing strangers: DANGER!

QUEENDUMB

Women of old had a fear of strangers and didn't date without a chaperone for they were smarter.

If this guy means right he'll go **ELSEWHERE** to get that money. Not to you, his future queen honey.

NO CHANCE OF LOOKING BAD

If a man wants to win a woman's heart and be her man he won't take any. chances of looking bad.

First he's asking for money then demanding to pimp you out. Know disrespect and see the louse.

Your gut rejects the guy before your frontal cortex if blinded by his great looks and appearance.

The minute you let him in, you've lost. It's like putting a python in your cage with no way out.

When I timidly begged for privacy they called me anti-social and I bought it, letting in the jackals.

Jackal: bad deeds done as follower or accomplice of another—they run together, birds of a feather.

DON'T LET EM IN/GO TO THE DOOR

Don't let em in, don't even go to the door, get a porch and screen that in, fence the yard, get a dog.

When vetting a partner, become even more restrictive in your screening, no fawning or cowering.

I'm lucky to be alive after all the people I foolishly let into my life. Screen them or die, aye.

A man truly interested won't open the relationship with a business proposition. Even if later, move on.

QUEENDUMB

A good man doesn't want to impress a potential partner with any wrong intentions, recall that son.

A strong/good man comes in to cover HER, never--ever--asking her to cover HIM. Never, ever.

WEASELLY

Anosognosia and her maladies: She finally realized she was doing it all to herself by smoking see.

Smoking is madness--oral cyclicity--but the only delivery system for pot cuz edibles are deadly.

Bulimia is recognized as a Fatal Mental Disorder with being bullied the reason for the behavior.

Weasely, that's all I can say. Asking her to put a good word/connections, it's always somethings see.

Is there ONE man on earth who just loves you for you? If you find him drop the jerks, more than a few.

You messed up with some dude and had sex. He then broached a business proposition--reject!

Do not consent to the rule of the despicable. You may fall into that outa survival fears you know.

When California went to hell I felt an evil shadow. When it affected people's moods I had to go.

Terse verse and timed rhymes, that's how I advance a new theory in psychology for all you guys.

The Only Escape

EVOLUTION OF MATURITY
OBSESSED WITH CREEPS
ESCAPE UNFAIR COMPARISONS
NOW YOUR DAYS ARE YOUR OWN
FEMALE SLAVE CONDITIONING
SHRINKING TO FIT HIM
GOAL: TO PLEASE GOD
ALONE: EVERY DAY'S PERFECT
HIX POLITIX

The Only Escape

EVOLUTION OF MATURITY

Before mature there's little you can do about your responses. You're possessed in a sense sis.

As you start to know self you gain self-control and are more insulated from these demons of hell.

Autonomisms: uncontrollable words and uprushes from the unconscious including social faux pas.

As I look back it's like another person acting out a script. A really weird one, no logic to it.

The YOU is missing, eclipsed by another or just soul smothered. Go solo for awhile, in prayer.

I walked around in a trance for decades feeling I was normal. I suffered then found God after all.

You let em in cuz you're stuck in sin. You have diverse lusts that attract em in, you being a trash bin.

Being a triple Pisces I was so sensitive you can't imagine the damage losing all perspective.

After incredible bedlam & trouble I landed in a cabin in the wilderness and the Potter made me over.

OBSESSED WITH CREEPS

THE ONLY ESCAPE

I got obsessed with creeps who didn't even deserve a conversation with this would-be queen.

The effects of involvement was sudden devastating failure but when I was alone, success forever.

These involvements were in my era of treason, when everyone and everything had gone wrong.

These were traumatized attachments: triggers of the early trauma and bloody fear of abandonment.

These were all involvements attracting into me, when I was vulnerable by my lack of boundaries.

Inferior attractions aren't let in when you're married, a wonderful wall you come behind happily.

Dust off your hands. Now don't go back or you'll spend another day under a grey cloud, trashed.

Creeps defined: Biblically they're trying to get into your house to hypnotize and use you til you die.

ESCAPE UNFAIR COMPARISONS

To escape unfair/mean comparisons, escape the matrix and get back into your own stream son.

It's as sure as pushing a button. You go there, you get hurt. You abstain [stay here], you end the curse.

If you don't go there, he can feel it. Think of that: just by doing nothing God vindicates the genius.

Going there is pulling a pain lever, not going there is like finding a new life with the True Self so clever.

You weren't even thining about age before you met him, degraded by living in his world of comparisons.

THE ONLY ESCAPE

Ageism took over your mind, feeling inferior just cuz you're older. It all goes away rid of this loser.

Some believe it, many are just misguided, most just jump on the bandwagon or lied about it.

You were weak then in an instant made yourself strong, just by deciding to not go there/go along.

Every time you went there you were beaten up. Mentally, emotionally, spiritually a dumb chump.

You hold the keys to happiness, not him. Just by not going there you're free, now continue on.

Reject this little man and expand: it'll happen at the same time cuz you did it--you became a woman.

Because you made this switch from living in a ditch to your self in full view, success comes in too.

NOW YOUR DAYS ARE YOUR OWN

Now every day's your own. That means 100% happy because you kicked that guy off the throne.

No more someone ruining your special days, just for the heck of it because it's written in his DNA.

No more crazy UPS and degrading, humiliating DOWNS. Every day happy now cuz you deleted a clown.

Association with people unproven or refusing to detach from toxic persons: this is not queendom.

People should be tonic not toxic. The Jezebels are trouble constant, the men are weakened by it.

Staying high on self is important cuz the devil is always dropping insults into your mind to block it.

THE ONLY ESCAPE

I need solitude to rediscover ME. It gets entwined, confused, mixed up and overshadowed see,

The social female values herself by relational status and forces people into her life who don't fit it.

My life was filled with traumatic experiences until I had a psychic opening into solitude and fences.

We contribute to our own trauma by never embracing seasons of solitude which are calling us.

How to walk away: wake-up to your own worth and accept the naked truth about this girl/guy.

To walk away, you must love yourself more and keep promises to yourself [to not go there anymore].

When she realized she controlled her own pain--by never going back again--she won/huge gain.

FEMALE SLAVE CONDITIONING

Thru female slave conditioning culture shrinks her self-perspective, in order to be manipulated.

Queens are never a man's secret. Secrets are shady and she could never live that way, forget it.

Any man asking you to keep a relationship secret is disrespectful. Never submit to this/be careful.

Men loved darkness more than light cuz their deeds were evil. Anyone like that is illegal or immoral.

Never be some inferior man's secret. His public acknowledgement is a must or avoid it.

Queens are never sexually swept away by flattery, a common trick of perverted male society.

THE ONLY ESCAPE

Sex is the original drug, a hallucinogenic. It hypnotizes the woman but the wrong man is the best at it.

She can't get rid of a man proven to be no good due to a sexual soul tie trashing her girlhood.

Millions of great women controlled by little men thru sexual means keeping them fogged, amen.

A man's use of time determines his priorities. See that if he calls you at the last minute always.

Never make a man your priority before he has clearly made you HIS. Don't ever be a fool sis.

Kings love women who have boundaries. Never cancel plans for a man if you want his respect honey.

Never shrink your profile to accommodate jealous intimidations. Be yourself & get away from him.

SHRINKING TO FIT HIM

If you have to miniaturize yourself to fit that guy's world then for heaven's sake don't do it girl.

He's comfortable at that level, fully extended. But you're compressed, no longer splendid.

If he's intimidated by your strength or success he thinks poorly of himself and may degrade you sis.

He's not enough man for you and he's unpredictable. You gotta shrink yourself and be hospitable.

Whether you forget him or not/stop his cruel taunts is totally up to you. Give that deep thought Sue.

Eject him and the pain you feel now will never be experienced again. This is heavenly relief man.

THE ONLY ESCAPE

Marry your vision, not a man feeling intimidation. Be as great as you can be, far in every direction.

Women aborting the vision God put in them [to accomodate some man] become harridans.

Harridan. A strict & bossy old woman. That's what I've become after suffering this bedlam.

My advice to you youngins: stand strong in your vision and esp. wait for better instead of sellin'.

Don't let em in & don't chase men. All you gotta do is grow spiritually then just smile/be a friend.

Wanting a man in your life can so consume you lose the vision God put in you and even get coo-coo.

GOAL: TO PLEASE GOD

Let your goal be to please God and manifest the fullness of what He's put in you, awed.

No-contact means no virtual links. Going there you're socked in the face/stabbed in the back see.

Mature in your talents then wait for God to send the right man to share your light: think about it.

A good man came by but the space was always filled cuz you weren't patient enough to wait girl.

If you appease people you get blamed rather than the true aggressors. Weakness is a real bummer.

You now have control, for it's YOU who determines your pain by either going there or staying away.

ALONE: EVERY DAY'S PERFECT

THE ONLY ESCAPE

By staying away every day's perfect. For it's determined by YOU not the petty retaliations of a nut.

Your days turned grey, always in reaction to what he say. How about you determining your day?

Don't give him a chance to sock your spirit. You going there is like lending him the knife to do it.

Getting older is not a running out of parts but a completion of more meaningful wholes. Jung

HIX POLITIX

You can't befriend them, you can't make deals with them. All you can do is bribe em to no end?

Risk-averse, overcautious, timid. It's a minimalist approach to foreign relations not to kill em.

This year we lost deterrence & adopted full scale appeasement and the world's in hell isn't it.

Free of Frenemies
[= HAPPY!]

MOST VALUABLE TIME IN LIFE
JUDGED BY HOW MANY FRIENDS
COLD HEARTS AND CLOUDED VISION
ANTISEMITISM AND DEMOCRATS/THE SQUAD
PUERILE PROTESTORS
EVIL SATANIC HATRED
I STILL CAN'T BELIEVE IT
NONRATIONAL MOVEMENTS
FALSE COMPARISONS TO MINIMIZE
LIE OF FALSE EQUIVALENCE
HISTORICAL MEMORY
LIGHTING A MATCH
FRIENDS AND ASSOCIATES
FRIENDS: ADD OR SUBTRACT?
STOIC WHILE CONNECTED
DEEPER ENGAGEMENT WITH SOCIETY

Free of Frenemies
[= HAPPY!]

When it comes to success it's not "if" but "when". Just relax, it's in the cards, it's your destiny friend.

Work: get the pettiness out of it and just work for the people. You'll be a success miss if no evil.

MOST VALUABLE TIME IN LIFE

These are such valuable times engaging with the inner self. I'm exhilarated by it/desire it above all.

Solitude is not an absence of company but a profound connection to self: fulfillment and tranquility.

I've been in solitude half my life now and it's obvious how petty people are, preventing your growth.

I love dogs but fear when I see one on the street. With mal-adaptation all can be violent see.

If you need people as a crutch, you know you need solitude to be happy with self/get a hunch.

JUDGED BY HOW MANY FRIENDS

The most beneficial thing in life is weeding friendships. It's a sudden exhilarating gain, not a loss.

We're judged by how many friends we have but people can be a hindrance, influenced by the masses.

FREE OF FRENEMIES

Right after the Oct 7 Jew slaughter she went in with Hamas, finding me horrible for being aghast.

We had no idea we had this abyss between us but both instantly knew we could not bridge it.

We now see each other as cold devils and that's how it will stay cuz we're both so strong willed.

All people are on probation as long as it's solitude [angels] you prefer above other interactions.

She always comes back, hat in hand. We happily chat then she's again taken in by leftist friends.

She weighs millions on her side and just a trickle on yours. You can't compete with this sir.

On the day you let her go, celebrate & throw a party! For every door closed there's five new entries.

COLD HEARTS AND CLOUDED VISION

The bad association clouded your vision. Reject the jerk to get a sudden enlightenment man.

If she can't see Oct 7 as stone age Satanism there's no talking to her, she sees em as freedom fighters.

Don't spend privacy time being angry how others trashed your privacy. Don't waste time see.

How could liberals, so focused on racism, be antisemitic? Just another contradiction, tragic.

ANTISEMITISM AND DEMOCRATS/THE SQUAD

Oct 7 terror attack globalized the intifada via the democrats led by the "squad" apparently.

FREE OF FRENEMIES

We have an institutionally antisemitic, pro-terrorist party--the democrats led by the squad see.

Anything Israel does to protect herself is condemned and Jew hatred around the world is common.

The response to Oct. 7 atrocity was jaw-dropping and I still can't accept it let alone the event itself.

Israel had it coming? Are you kidding? Little babies burned alive/put in ovens: it was sadism see.

PUERILE PROTESTORS

Queers for Palestine? I can't think of a more contradictory idea but that's the kids, aye.

We would not have ended any such brutality had we not fought to win, but that's not how it's been.

The democratic party: an unprincipled organization seeking power for those who run it. Mark Levin

Liberal news media like New York Post is the propaganda wing for Hamas in the United States.

Islamaphobia? Where are all the marching Jews demanding the obliteration of all Muslims?

It's holocaust relativism and atrocity denialism. To prevent war, watch these dangerous trends.

Jews are appalled at the left's normalization of anti-Jewish rhetoric, but will they change? Heck

Stats show college kids are lonelier, more depressed, lack friends and are addicted to porn/drugs.

So of course they could be for terrorists/Hamas who dismember children in front of their parents.

FREE OF FRENEMIES

These are subhuman animals and the kids love them. This has brought truth out as a silver lining.

Democrats have created an inhumane generation and change is blocked since hearts are hardened.

Any efforts to change the hardened hearts of youth will take time, effort and BIG changes here too.

The more sensitive you are the more messed up without Jesus. Only the persecuted sees this.

EVIL SATANIC HATRED

Antisemitism: A cruel Satanic spirit FLARING UP in dark times, an evil hatred from the depths, aye.

It's like blaming a rape victim: even before Israel retaliated they were ELATED/cheered em on.

It's like it's always simmering beneath but then it's triggered to a worldwide evil hatred see.

The Nazi type in 1930 spread its net to include all dark people and then the marginal like homosexuals.

Because she refused to condemn the sadism of Oct. Seven we'll never talk again, a giant schism.

To actually find moral equivalence between outright sadism & collateral damage is morally foolish.

It's jaw dropping how fast Jew-hatred took over after baby-killing sadism cheered by liberal losers.

I STILL CAN'T BELIEVE IT

I still can't believe it, no thinking person can. Then they realize: yes I can, it happened way back then.

FREE OF FRENEMIES

Acres and acres of corpses--they wanted to kill every single Jew. Old, young, poor or the rich too.

It's in their charter darn it: to wipe out Israel and every Jew. Sadism takes over with the citizens too.

Your trusted friend's sudden flare-up on the side of Hamas, disregarding Oct 7: it's SATAN friends.

There are irrational movements not based on logic or facts. Never minimize the danger of mass.

Non-rational movements can kill millions. Forget facts or logic, just mind social psychology son.

NONRATIONAL MOVEMENTS

Once a non-rational movement takes off it can't be blocked cuz they censure all that's not.

The massive protestors don't know what they're talking about. It's like gossip, there's no disputing it.

It's a tsunami of Jew-hatred across America see. It's very concerning because it's incendiary.

In the eyes of majors we come off like an annoying ex-girlfriend rather than leader of the free world.

It's about October Seventh and the masks it removed. About the universities, friends and family too.

To UNPACK what October Seventh identified takes great strength to face facts on genocide.

The Holocaust could not have happened had the state of Israel existed. That's how massive this is.

When it comes to friends let the reaction to Oct. 7 be the litmus test. It reveals all about em sis.

FREE OF FRENEMIES

The entire west must collapse from within. That's the destructive impulse you see with Dems in.

The false binary--oppressor vs. oppressed--can be transmuted to any form for evil purposes.

Powerlessness does not equal moral decency but that's how the progressives view Palestine see.

Hamas is a condemned terrorist organization in America yet Stanford/the ivy leaguers love it.

How can you educate people in these marches when it's about hatred and lack of history read?

They are friends of enemies of Jewish people, and thus freedom in the only democracy there too.

FALSE COMPARISONS TO MINIMIZE

Where victims rule "holocaust envy" takes over: they're jealous of status of the worst victims ever.

False comparisons to minor genocides chips away at the MAJOR one which they're sure to deny.

The liberal trend is to dismantle the truth of the holocaust itself by including everything/all.

"The holocaust wasn't that unique and Jews should shut up about it". Holocaust denialism is illegit.

They brand all terrible events as genocide. They were bad but no comparison to when 6 mil. died.

The new antisemitism is to be jealous of the King of Victims so they deny it all or ignore em.

THE LIE OF FALSE EQUIVALENCE

FREE OF FRENEMIES

They falsely compare Palestine to WWII Warsaw—much brainwashing like this comes from Hamas.

No more holocaust memorial day unless "other" genocides are included--this also chips away.

Denying the holocaust or the savagery of Oct. 7 shows a hardened heart so best to sever connection.

It's the Lie of Moral Equivalence. You see this on the news, false comparisons to support Hamas.

Truth: an apocalyptically violent movement of Jew haters has declared war on Israel/U.S./the west.

It's longstanding hatred always finding it's way back thru contemporary issues borrowed from it.

With a long history of pasting blame on Jews, that's what they reach for when things fall through.

Jew hatred appears in dark times like a downturn of enlightenment values, a crisis of reason too.

When people turn away from truth, reason and moral clarity is when antisemitism comes out ok.

Having a scapegoat for problems allows them to not look for rational solutions based on reason.

HISTORICAL MEMORY

There is an Historical Memory of jew hatred. It's a racial hypnotic and easy way not to look at self.

Civilization is on the line this moment: we're barbarians going down if Oct. 7 we can't condemn it.

Will we defend democracy or an incredibly reactionary, racist, backward movement run by savagery?

FREE OF FRENEMIES

I hate how they kill our children but I hate even more how they make us kill theirs. Golda Meir

Oct. 7 and even more reactions to it have opened the lid to something none of us ever expected.

At this important junction we must speak up for the values of western civilization or we're done.

LIGHTING A MATCH

Brainwashed: Oct 7 lit a match on worldview they already had from the commie professors, bad.

"Freedom fighters" don't commit the sadistic acts they did, horrors when all civilization is now dead.

10-7: I'm happy it flushed em out. That's the one silver lining as I needed to weed my friendship garden.

Fukkem, kick em to the road. This is too much of a chasm between us, they're uncivilized and cold.

Oct 7 forces you to look at all your friends in a new way, questioningly. It's the new litmus test ok.

The callous jerks see that sadism as "resistance" and it makes me choke and gasp, I'm aghast.

FRIENDS AND ASSOCIATES

"Tranquility in virtue" has much to say about the friendships we forge & company we keep too.

We should foster connections in harmony with our <u>deepest values</u> or life turns rough and crude.

A handful of genuine connections outweighs a plethora of superficial ones, and you can be alone.

173

FREE OF FRENEMIES

Being "social" is building your house on shifting sands depending on what's going on with humans.

The need for many friends reflects one's unsteady sense of self relying on approval or else.

Inner peace is our best companion as a need for extensive outer validation slows way down.

When healthy we carefully select relationships which are complementary to our inner serenity.

I discovered many friends to be a terrible drain, as nothing's more productive than solitude ok.

FRIENDS: ADD OR SUBTRACT?

I discovered "friends" as expectations and interruptions and increasingly dropped off all connections.

Walking on eggs so I wouldn't trigger her: that wasn't a authentic friendship I discovered later.

My way to happy freedom was to not have friends. No expectations, disappointments, vacillations.

I discovered women to be rigid thinkers and virtue signalers. Sorry girls, also social whores.

Happy when alone. Must be strong enough to discount the world calling you a hideous old crone.

They actually judge worth by how many social connections one has and what a dreary path.

By being content inside ourselves we form friendships which are not crutches but enhancements.

Eating disorders fall into the same generation as dysfunctional families since trauma is the basis.

FREE OF FRENEMIES

STOIC WHILE CONNECTED

Remaining stoic while connected prevents the potential emotional chaos of external environments.

When your happiness is within you will not be subjected to the tides of social whims.

Stoics engage socially but remain watchful that such activities don't bring stress or distraction.

I tailored every word to suit/avoid triggering her cuz that meant she would leave--what a bummer.

She controlled the narrative that way and the entire relationship. Fortunately I finally saw that.

The stoic can give a meaningful contribution to society while never being at the mercy of it, finally.

DEEPER ENGAGEMENT WITH SOCIETY

This enables a deeper engagement with society but on one's own terms--what a breath of fresh air.

I was constantly hurt in social interactions even with family: a stranger in a strange land feeling.

If she can never think outa the box or it threatens her that you do, something to think about Sue.

She started out as a narcissist with a diva complex but with liberalism she became the witchiest.

It's not the amount of friends one has but the depth of virtue they bring into your life. Stoic view

Solitude is not a void but a fertile ground for personal introspection. Most lives remain unexamined.

FREE OF FRENEMIES

The answer to depression is taking control finally. It's being in between, the unqueen which is sickly.

Once high again now STAY ON TOP. How to do that: don't go back, don't compare, never stop.

Body's not made for constant anxiety living with a narc. With unpredictability you'll never be a star.

NO LURKING
[and other unqueenly things]

BREAKUPS
HATE AND SECOND RATE STATUS
RADICAL UNTRUTHS OF YOUTH
THE PRESSURE TO ACCULTURATE
PEOPLE PROBLEMS
MENTAL ILLNESS
OPPRESSION OLYMPICS
AMERICAN VALUES
INEVITABLE CATASTROPHES
ANTISEMITISM IN EVERY GENERATION
THE IRONY OF JEW-HATRED
RESOLVING CONTRADICTIONS

NO LURKING
[and other unqueenly things]

BREAKUPS

Breakups: If you lurk you'll feel like a second rate jerk. Get into your own stream, remove his curse.

You lose your queen status/royalty every time you lurk, making them big in perception/come first.

Withdraw all energy/focus into yourself now. Let him fade, decouple, go deep inside/have a ball.

Just by you going there it's like your nose is pushed up to the glass, feeling inferior, ignored, less.

Don't let em rent-free in your head! Don't you see you're wasting time/you need to go on ahead.

I know what it's like to have second rate status, I lived that way for years. It just came naturally sir.

HATE AND SECOND RATE STATUS

So you felt hated. Transfer this to what the Jews felt throughout history: the relief of commonality.

You don't take hate so personally when you see the commonality, in fact it dulls the blade.

See your depression as rooted in the environment, including what and WHO you think about.

Their hatred was a painful arrow and she became obsequious, increasing their hate/her sorrow.

NO LURKING

Responding to hate with obsequiousness [servile fawning] triggers more viciousness darling.

I didn't have to tools to do anything but curl up in a ball, terrified but not knowing how to stop my fall.

I had never met people like that--mom never prepared me for such crap--but then I got a new map.

The women were the worst. I didn't know how to respond to female bullies, and what a curse.

This cowering attitude becomes a kind of people-worship based on Stockholm Syndrome, ick.

I overcame them and gained strength in resistance thru prayer and fasting, building a battleship.

The third device was staying away: never allow trauma bonds to develop and to LOVE HOME all day.

If you can't say what you want around someone--curbing your speech--you block energy see.

RADICAL UNTRUTHS OF YOUTH

The youth/kids are barbaric ok. They scream like toddlers or have silly tantrums to get their way.

Radical untruths are the animating principals for violent group tantrums: MOBBISM triggering millions.

The basic 101 of Social Psychology: it's all a herd which sees truth as each other, nothing other.

The superior man has his own reality while the neurotic herd man takes on the group reality only.

The individual thinker, God's man, is likely to be miserably misjudged when with herd men.

NO LURKING

He marches to his own drum, they're hypnotized by the bovine group beat which is dumbed down.

To think your own thoughts is an achievement of a very few. But to do this you need boundaries Sue.

It's another way of saying: the individual is right, the group is always wrong, and this is relieving.

THE PRESSURE TO ACCULTURATE

The pressure is to acculturate: adopt, adapt, become one with, conform and there's no trouble ok.

The narcissist group will fight your boundaries. There's gonna be a pushback & you better be ready.

Many of you are intimidated by barbaric kids. By being so you're setting them up as pre-convicts.

I see Stockholm Syndrome in grannies. She loves everything he does and never punishes see.

He hits her up for money and intimidates her physically. Every time she gives in he gets more surly.

It was anarchy-in-conformity. They came in groups then demanded I agree with them perfectly.

They had no fathers/were raised by feminist mothers so what could you expect other than losers?

Aliens walking in, another generation filled with pride and sin, made me sick/not my friends.

Truth be damned, the tribe is king. From veritas [truth] to barbaros in ivy league schools unbelievably.

Defense of barbaric brutality has swept the academic world cuz they're cold and callous you know.

NO LURKING

Gouging baby's eyes out: professors called a "stunning victory" and "exhilarating"--evil/crazy.

Lord sustains the fatherless and widow. He heals the brokenhearted & binds their wounds too.

At one point the Jews were forced to disperse and live around strangers. This was a curse I wager.

PEOPLE PROBLEMS

They'll rage at you behind the wheel but if you get outa the car they'll talk you back gently see.

The neighbor's needs always come before yours with the covert narc--it's society's approval he's after.

First he scammed me, then I told him I knew it, then I got married and everyone knows he blew it.

I prefer sleeping bags on tables not sheets and beds: another example of how traditions are shed.

Mom: the ease with which she'd pull out her heavy artillery was so intimidating we all caved in.

The key to success is patience. You can't make it happen and cannot quicken true success.

MENTAL ILLNESS

In the past I said mentally ill things and acted in mentally ill ways: something we all can say.

Don't be jealous of me unless you're willing to go thru/do what I did to get it. Joyce Meyers

The mere fact you put up with them means you still needed the lesson so good for that too son.

NO LURKING

When I discovered how happy I was alone it changed it all as everyone else was now on probation.

As an elder you have much to say which the youth NEVER HEAR. Speak up/they need you dear.

Don't bemoan what you went thru in bootcamp, the humiliation and pain of learning all that.

Don't bemoan what you went thru in bootcamp, the humiliation and pain of learning all that.

Liberals have a built-in inoculation against listening to anyone disagreeing so give up on that thing.

OPPRESSION OLYMPICS

They see only "oppressed" and "oppressors" so ANYTHING you do to the latter is legit sir.

Hamas: Without chaos it cannot survive but in horror and darkness this is how they thrive.

They justify baby killing with "Israel deserves it". More than anything this reveals callousness

Your friends who can't condemn Oct. 7: it's a measure of their callousness, they can't even see em.

They want countries who are used to tyranny and guns banned for self-defense, most importantly.

It's the most ancient hatred and oldest form of discrimination: Jew hatred/antisemitism.

Multiculturalism means all value systems are equal: this absurdity is obvious to any intellectual.

If we can't distinguish between value systems then there's no distinction between all men.

NO LURKING

Diversity in race/ethnicity is strength only if values are the same. Mutual values = differences ok.

My neighbor is an Arab Muslim but Americanized and hey, our values are the SAME you guys.

He wants what we all want: freedom, small government out of our pocket, low taxes and protected.

AMERICAN VALUES

What are unAmerican values? High taxes, government control, low military and defunded police too.

The most unAmerican value is open borders--and high walls indicates DISGUST because it must.

Krazy Kollege Kids gotta go to another country to see what it's like or just watch WWII docs, aye.

Intermarriage brought those brutal values into the system and we all collapsed into alcoholism.

The left destroys a city, the right builds it back up again then the left destroys it again. Maga wisdom

They're inoculated against listening for even five minutes to a different view so stay coo-coo.

Back then every country had slaves so the issue is: how was America different? She freed them ok.

Cosmic joke: The highest IQ countries are the ones agreeing that men menstruate/have babies.

An inanity: why English speaking countries have bought toxic stupidity more than others see.

Why are jews democrats? Cuz they mis-associate the right with the Nazis and the left with morality.

NO LURKING

I never ask myself: will the truth upset the left? For it's worth it if they come around and be blessed.

Jews should know they aren't voting for FDR but for the dems of the 21st century, a Jew-hating scare.

INEVITABLE CATASTROPHES

The inevitable happens when you let people in your country who don't share your values see.

In the 80's it was seen as the sweet thing to do: let alot of people in who don't share your values.

In left-wing hearts there's a desire to destroy America as we know it. Our prosperity: they hate it.

Letting the unvetted millions in is one example of America-hate instilled by evil forces ok.

Vast conservative immigration? The left would ban em, it's only those easily bought to vote for them.

Why do they fear too many Cubans coming in? Because they've had it with communism.

The most foolish/destructive doctrines for 100 years is "man is good" even the leftists in Hollywood.

"Man is good" jargon was central to the enlightenment or "age of reason"--a giant contradiction.

ANTISEMITISM IN EVERY GENERATION

Ignored fact: Palestinian Authority tells children their highest calling is to kill Jews/take their land.

The West is in moral chaos. In the US if you say men can't give birth you may lose your job sis.

NO LURKING

Is antisemitism in every generation not proof of God and His chosenism? A provocative question.

Evil focuses on Jews first, never the Jews last. It's not like decent people wanted them gassed.

THE IRONY OF JEW-HATRED

The irony of Jew-hatred is that it validates the chosenness of the Jews: think about that too.

I'm wondering if the elect has similar problems of persecution for unknown reason, you think?

When people hear Jew-hatred they don't often ask "why"--they just assume an ugly reason, aye.

People adopt Jew-hatred cuz it's primal, biblical, deeper than hell and as always, SOCIAL.

This whole thing is so obvious you'd have to go to college to deny it. Dennis Prager.

Biggest problem is me, sitting here. But in secular schools we learn the biggest problem is America.

For superior selfix and looks always fast on Sundays. To fine tune a fine engine, gotta do it one day.

RESOLVING CONTRADICTIONS

What's written in my DNA/skillset/talent sheet is the compulsion to resolve contradiction see.

If you find your steam pressure with cocky self-assertion than that's what you should do son.

I did the work: I completed my assignment on earth. Now I"m waiting with anticipation [worth].

NO LURKING

The key to your success is patience. You've already asked God now kindly give His plans a chance.

Teach your children that self-control is infinitely more important than self-esteem. Dennis Prager

If you had known it you wouldn't have gone thru it so count it up to another necessary canyon.

If the bitter path of experience ends with the noble path of reflection I'd say it was a life well done.

The older human knows he's gonna die so doesn't put up with things like those time-wasting guys.

BULLY FASTING

DANGEROUS FAMILY BULLIES
FEMALE BULLIES THE WORST
DELIBERATE HUMILIATION
BEWARE OF EVIL HELPERS
DOMINANT ANIMALS
ANGER PUSHBACK
BORN IN THE FIRE
JEALOUS AND POWER-HUNGRY
DON'T LOOK BACK
ABANDON ALL SOUL TIES
SOCIETAL FLARE UPS
DIVINE FAST DAY
FACE DISTRUST OR BUST
STOP STUFFING FROM OUTSIDE
YOUR CALLING AS A SPEAKER
IT'S LONELY AT THE TOP

THE BULLY FAST

DANGEROUS FAMILY BULLIES

There's a women-hating strain in both sexes and she who overcomes this hex is queen/a Mrs.

Our canyons teach us what we need for success if we're not blocked by PTSD from the sad events.

Today is your victory over yourself/yesterday, tomorrow is your victory over lesser men. Musashi

The bully tries to control the perception of the target by the group or masses. She's a gossip/calumnious.

A bully puts a label on you and turns all against you too, getting more intense until breakthrough.

A bully sibling can knock you out of a family. This kinda thing is a most common form of treachery.

One consequence of sin is being in the grip of forces beyond our control making one ugly/old.

FEMALE BULLIES THE WORST

The female bully will get everyone to hate her estranged husband or hate her sister the odd one.

A bully has GOT to put you down to keep his place in the foreground: it's the history of humans.

BULLY FASTING

She didn't want anyone to think well of me, a lowlife. Feeling power she wanted annihilation, aye.

Rejecting a bully is dangerous. They get predictably vindictive, inciting violence/disinheriting us.

When rejecting/disentrenching from bullies have a backup plan, support and fence up/wall in.

As we become more aware, fear grows. Keep in mind you wanted the bully around/you didn't know.

Now you know what you know, you're well-protected with no reason to fear, allowing growth.

DELIBERATE HUMILIATION

Bully: it's a pattern of repeated and deliberate humiliation of others: the smaller/weaker/younger.

Any target forms a complex of rejection and a sense of being lost/inferior, a stranger in a strange land.

Repeated degradation of one's identity can track his development into gutter grooves see.

The targeting of those with less power distinguishes bullying from common aggression/mobbing.

They try to change minds. Bullying tries to change perceptions of one, without which he'd be fine.

Humans are social animals, part of the pack. Rejected they die of starvation or take on a new map.

The bully uses this human need against the target: let us ostracize him from the pack darn it
.
I suffered bullying for years and felt a sick stomach and black cloud the entire time with nightly tears.

BULLY FASTING

The female bully wouldn't shut up and spent all day on the phone wrecking my rep. Jezebel spirit.

BEWARE OF EVIL HELPERS

She'd offer to help me but beware of evil helpers. They just want a foot in to destroy your life further.

Bullying peaks at 14 then childlike behavior wanes, but many adults act more like children every day.

With young kids it's kicking/hitting/shoving. With adult kids it's reputation-wrecking/gossiping.

Relational aggression--damaging relationships--is far more common as evil children grow older.

Spreading rumors and social exclusion: how common and how hurtful this device of generations.

Bullying gives short term results when they lack the social skills to attain without hurting folks.

DOMINANT ANIMALS

Since bullying is a device for dominance, without social skills it can turn very primal/ugly: violence.

They want to smash, silence, dim the light of, destroy perceptions of a target tho' gentle as a dove.

You're in a group feeling power and love. A bully hates this and starts this process like a kid's shove.

Entering a new domain we must prepare to meet the bullies. The new kid on the block they hate see.

If people see you rising they'll knock you down. Hard facts about humans are a must for the crown.

BULLY FASTING

When they're the ones with the power to do so, you're strapped with your own wisdom to grow.

ANGER PUSHBACK

You can't get angry, pushback. Can't scream and yell in a tantrum, locked up. It's URGENT to grow up.

Bullies take sadistic pleasure in taking down the weak. It's in their nature like some animals see.

If a target of bullies they can take all one has, destroy his relationships and block all his plans.

All groups differ by threshold levels bringing reaction. For some it's so rigid you're just killed son.

They could hurt you, put you outa business, shrewdly screw you in a will, even make you homeless.

BORN IN THE FIRE

It happened to me, apparently born a threat to everyone. I learned to expect tribulation.

One weak bully can cause an entire family to hate your guts--like a brilliant speaker called a klutz.

Truth tellers, insight revealers and God lovers are all common targets of the mean bully's gall.

I'm telling you this for if aware of what's going on you can hold on: to your stuff, peace, reputation.

Bullying is TYRANNY. Bullying makes you lose your free expression which is now blocked by them.

It's all about a power differential and they're suddenly bothered by your divine calling that's all.

JEALOUS AND POWER-HUNGRY

BULLY FASTING

The jealous, envious power-hungry humans are the problem and your obstacle to overcome.

If the siblings have more power than you they can really harm and take all they want too.

They destroy the target financially but the worst and most common is the hurting him emotionally.

They wanna dictate the feelings of others and hurt you for sport, taking great joy in it of course.

A bully's fed by your reaction and he LOVES to see you grovel. Preplan all dealings with him/stand tall.

Since they're bottom feeders, the more your reaction the more they're fed, these treacherous stingers.

DON'T LOOK BACK

I humbly beseech you Lord for people are too dumb to talk to, won't listen & are getting violent too.

The key to world success is getting LESS into them and MORE into you—the opposite to their view.

Because you did not take care of it then, going back is counterproductive since you're ever-losin'.

Instead of going back, thank God for all you learned from these painful lessons & accept facts.

Don't go back cuz it's never resolved. It just triggers adrenalin and hatred, all success blocked.

I take full responsibility for bringing on their bad reactions by my actions. That's kinda it son.

Never despise small beginnings and never remorse over your painful trainings by inferior weaklings.

BULLY FASTING

You've been dealing with a closed mind so this recent rupture's predictable: learn from it or die.

I admire her, I'll be sorry when she passes too but I still can't give up my own interests or afternoons.

The mere fact you went thru it shows you still had to learn it and that explains painful minutes

Don't look back or turn into an old salt statue. You're to go on ahead not return to the old school.

Those who are desperate for love make it hardest to love em cuz it's the same original trauma.

The world is full of mean people today. Is it cuz they're evil or just hurting? Either way, stay away.

She didn't pass moral litmus test [do you condemn Oct 7?] so you've split from this & are blessed.

Don't bemoan bad past. To come this high you experienced deep canyons first, that's the map.

Academia has succumbed to consequentialism: truth is legit if it doesn't hurt one groups feelings.

ABANDON ALL SOUL TIES

Abandon the soul tie, walk away--and very soon you won't see what you ever saw in that guy.

Wicked bands of control, mixed signals and jealousy triangles, pack murder of one over all.

Musing while looking out the window is more productive than forcing things ya know.

A bully's perception of you causes others to harm you. A seemingly harmless aunt will do this too.

BULLY FASTING

The bully seeks to isolate and get you away from protection. Don't dare get in his car son.

A bully wants us all to have a bad opinion of you. He'll stop at nothing like a wrecking ball fool.

In the case of two bully sisters against one, it's a matrix which never changes til one dies son.

In a case of two bully sisters in Cinderella syndrome with mom, better fast til the prince comes.

A bully is habitually cruel and insulting. A black cloud formed whenever my sister started her ranting.

The two had a leg up against one in a vice grip they'd never let go of but with God you won.

SOCIETAL FLARE UPS

Black teens beating up old white male busdrivers who are fired if they dare fight back: race wars.

Race wars are starting and I'd get fenced up/the hell away quickly, esp with antisemitism see.

Antisemitic FLARE UPS as race wars START UP. Hitler's hatred spreads to other groups/look it up.

People that we knew/had a lot in common with are suddenly antisemitic and seeming callous.

AMA said "don't list sex of newborns for they may change later". Insanity is endless/depthless sir.

Any comic for free speech/the amendments is seen as a Trumper and fired as a consequence.

DIVINE FAST DAY

BULLY FASTING

See your fast day--your trump card when troubled--as a blast, party, cosmic journey, the key ok.

Get outa the gut and keep the energy high in the head: the way to solve problems and go on ahead.

When troubled eating solves nothing but to block your energy. You can't digest anyway.

Trouble days are opportunities to pass the test. Make gold: refuse to use old devices of the past.

Fasting is a divine strategy which always works so congratulations on this day--is it your first?

You had to find this divine trump card so thank God for troubles taking you here going forward.

On my first fast day in the midst of a blitz my mood changed instantly and the answer came fast.

FACE DISTRUST OR BUST

Answer: she couldn't trust anyone in her entire family and strangely this relieved her suddenly.

In the fast you reach a point where you don't want to eat, you don't want to ever break it or cheat.

As long as I fast I'm the prince, the king, the queen or anything else I dam want to be sweetie.

Just say: Today is my day to create a new reality, to live in a dream and to make it all come true see.

Just for today you win out over all enemies, just cuz they're low [ever eating] and you're high see.

"Lord, WHEN will you help me?" And He said "are you fasting today? Then it'll be today sweetie."

BULLY FASTING

How to cure your ulcers: Fast until nausea is gone then eat only meat and soon they're gone sir.

Eating meat becomes part of your body. There's your simple cure due to what we call biosimilarity.

STOP STUFFING FROM OUTSIDE

Stop stuffing info from the outside and instead increase your fidelity for a superior journey inside.

Increase your fidelity, your amplitude. To get the maximum from the outer and the inner too.

It is not a waste to just sit and think. These times are the most productive so seclude then see.

Meditation is just looking out the window, waiting like a cat watching a mouse hole: for a miracle.

Some things need a fast to trigger them. These are most exciting, far-reaching discoveries of men.

YOUR CALLING AS A SPEAKER

Practice your speech then RELAX. Let it seep in, don't force it, return to the script, relax again.

Do as Einstein did: He saw mental pictures, not linear concepts. Visualize it first then SPEAK it.

See everything in mental pictures then jot down a few words. It's as simple as that, now come first.

Don't panic over this speaking thing, it is be a pleasant experience if you're truly called to do it.

You KNOW somethings gonna happen cuz your work is done and you see breakthrough patterns.

BULLY FASTING

Whenever you hit a glitch, fast or cut carbs: i.e. do something different to trigger a switch.

Do something different. For a workaholic that means taking a break so new openings show a way.

IT'S LONELY AT THE TOP

There's a reason loneliness comes with success. The superior man rises HIGH above the mess.

Most people are intellectually lazy. They just repeat things they hear from a group or family.

Separate from the crowd or the Dunning-Kruger Effect takes over: dumbed down and loud.

They hate you thru their leftist-warped eyes. You've done nothing wrong but still they despise.

You could not have made it out there before now, you were too angry. Now you're dignified see.

FAST TO SEE/BE FREE

They pinned something on you which was so unfair and they'll pay dearly for their calumny dear.

Self-forgive for your lower self. This is a main obstacle so be a success by passing this major test.

I went way up, got a taste of it. Then I went WAY down for my Ph.D. in the Streets before leadership.

Tho' I could do nothing, my biggest fear was the past. I'd relive it with a full adrenalin/cortisol blast.

God said not to fear evil but the world brings me fear even still. Only in solitude do I feel real.

Fast on food, fast on him, fast on everything. See it as a party: subtraction not addition, just be lazy.

DEALING WITH CRIMINAL MINDS

Bullies have criminal minds: fear, shaming and humiliation. They want you down, beneath them.

Bullies lose power as you refuse to cower. Deep down they don't deserve respect & they know it.

When they bombard don't counterpunch. Go grey rock until your come back then speak/be staunch.

Never react emotionally, it's giving them what they want: supply, the utter thrill of hurting thee.

Bullies operate by keeping their victim alone and powerless. Stay connected, call your friends.

Remember he has no power other than your fear. Stay cool until time to spring up/escape King Lear.

FAST TO SEE/BE FREE

An assertive unemotional response lets bully know you won't be victimized yet don't pose a challenge.

THE FEMALE BOOTCAMP

Overcoming bully is a woman's boot camp. Assertion is salvation or you'll be run over/enslaved fast.

Anyone with ambition must learn how to deal with one. Learn assertion or life will be obstruction.

A challenge gives bully the attention and power he's seeking so be smart with pseudo-agreeing.

They want you to cry and complain so don't engage. The keyword here is to WAIT then escape.

Challenge a bully and he won't say anything but the next day you'll find your cat missing.

The devil waits and he lurks in patience--waiting for that opening to take you down perchance?

Your attitude should be: "if that's how you wanna be go ahead but I'm gonna move on", said in calm.

FORGIVE THO' ANGRY

It's hard to forgive with righteous anger inside but it's easy if you see the lifesaving lessons, aye.

Silently thank your brutal captors in the past. They made you great and a leader at last.

Stay professional, don't let em get under your skin. Be prepared to respond swiftly without fightin'.

Be a lady/straightforward: "I don't think your tone is appropriate": using the velvet glove on idiots.

FAST TO SEE/BE FREE

You went mute so they took over but now you're back and that's alot of coal on their head: fact.

Don't let people take over cuz they're not equipped. If you let em prepare for bedlam/getting sick.

To get their approval you gave them authority and the whole enterprise was demolished see.

FAKE CONSERVATIVE WOMEN

Who's calling you a nut--is she drinking all day, watching CNN, on the phone ever gossiping?

She says she's conservative but she's liberal as she can be. Happily, this revealed itself recently.

Don't be dumb, watch tell tale signs like virtue signaling, sitting around doing nothing, dreams of traveling.

She rests on her laurels while daily she does nothing but fret over people problems/gossiping.

When he called Hamas "brothers" I was shocked but realized of course he'd conform to the mob.

Ulcer regimens say NO RED MEAT but recent carnivore studies show it's red meat curing the ulcer see?

YOU'VE REACHED THE RAZOR'S EDGE

You've reached a point where you MUST FAST. There's too much to be done/to be overcome.

You're on the razor's edge: between complete world success vs. humiliating failure/the dregs.

Regard that guy/the soul tie as a previous era which is ghosted in mind cuz you took control, aye.

FAST TO SEE/BE FREE

Don't give him any energy and thank God you're able to let him go and start a brand new life happily.

Cure: stop cowering before men [embarrassed for living] and bust through to preeminence instead.

Don't ever again degrade yourself by going back to his page. You may as well see his ugly face.

If he chose another [new supply] it's a better reason never to see him, like you never knew him.

IT HAD TO HAPPEN THAT WAY

To reconcile the past: you had to do it to learn the lessons that would have prevented it, alas.

I wouldn't have gone thru it had I known, for only that pain taught me the lessons of the throne.

Without boundaries I was defined by whatever was in front of me, a rudderless ship of misery.

Only with high walls/strict boundaries am I free to flourish in uniqueness: right to be quirky.

The past is but a dimension: of lowness. Lower self-esteem, dignity, boundaries, understandings.

Looking back you can see how the trauma bond manifested in your life/insanity, blindly.

All that yelling you did, was this not the primal scream of an accused child against all they said?

A falsely accused person feels WILD inside and without proper training can really screw up his life.

TO ISOLATES AND NERDS

FAST TO SEE/BE FREE

Realize with pride your differences being alone all your life and them so social, wasting their time.

What makes it worse is liberals always accuse others of what THEY do/did and it really makes ya sick.

Invite God to your project and it'll be made whole miraculously as the angels surround thee.

Realize your differences studying/creating all your life while they were busily socializing, aye.

Realize your uniqueness marching to your own drum in isolation while they're conformists/dumb.

Once you see your radical differences your anxiety ends when it comes to speaking to them.

You've got something so valuable to give to them, having marched to a different drum, amen.

The best talents ripen LATE so don't let em put you down for doing your thing at an elder age.

Here you were so proud/so well read and now you hear they've been spreading vile stories instead.

MADMAN/SAVIOR ARCHETYPE

It's the nigredo stage of making gold: realizing that indeed you were a madman then letting it go.

The exalted savior archetype begins as a madman, so see it that way/feel proud you overcame man.

What made you so insane? All your energy mal-adapting to THEM but they don't see it that way.

Their reality was so mixed up as long as you were adapting to it your personality was messed up.

FAST TO SEE/BE FREE

"And I was so hurt by so many people through the years and no one cares." Old lady woes

Their reality was so mixed up as long as you were adapting to it your personality messed up.

The left leaning approach to crime has turned the cities into shit holes yet still they're given votes.

THE OVERCOMING BULLY FAST

Every time you endure a hunger pain you show God how much you love Him and a reward is coming.

Self-control is a fruit of the spirit and your girl doesn't have it. Any little craving, she gives into it.

Hunger pain makes me smile cuz I know reward follows sacrifice. Good, sacrifice is what they despise.

They'll call your fasting anorexic--a put down cuz they can't/don't wanna do it. Ignore these idiots.

God said WHEN we fast, not IF. It's a divine device and something we all should CRAVE to do sis.

How to cure your ulcers: Fast until nausea is gone then eat only meat and soon you're well sir.

Bully-fasting will go down in history because that's what it's about as war tool: overcoming.

The world is all for bullies, they own it for Satan's about domination but we have the fasting remedy.

I will endure hunger pain Lord, kindly notice. I trust in your words that rewards follow sacrifice.

Whatever we did--whether a wild toot or just buttered popcorn--fasting reverts to perfection sis.

FAST TO SEE/BE FREE

FASTING IS THE HERO'S PATH

Fasting is part of Hero's Path, the greatest prize hard to attain, the winner's main device, the last test.

Pineapple seems so pure but on my ulcer it was like gas on an open wound and I screamed in fear.

Eating plants with self-protective mechanisms: that was the basis of my intestinal defections.

Painful stickers all over the ground here: the plant's self-defense to keep themselves pure.

Bully fasting: cuz it's always about overcoming but the world handles obstructions thru sinning.

It's hard to believe meat is the cure since we've been told we should fear cuz it causes cancer.

Whiskey and steak with occasional morning pancakes: the cowboy diet and they were handsome ok.

Adding carbohydrate to the carnivore diet means heartburn, bloat and nausea and I proved it.

CONTROLLERS ARE ILL EQUIPPED

Being wrong wasn't a bad thing if you learned about people and learning to stay away from evil.

The terrifying thing about them taking control is they're not equipped and it means your FALL.

Act quickly & consistently son. The longer bully has power over you the stronger his hold becomes.

Someone taking over is an invasion of an enemy into your hard won territory. Be a leader quickly.

FAST TO SEE/BE FREE

Some feckless idiot as your emissary? It's a stupid way to be: gotta be careful who talks for thee.

He's a snake so if you don't stand up for your rights the aggression worsens. Keep this thought hon'.

Sometimes all you gotta do is wait awhile. Get outa the heat of the moment, cool heads, no guile.

Wait awhile as the enemy implodes naturally. Never interfere while he's destroying himself see.

The clashing of temperaments can stick in your craw for years, but it was just principalities & powers dear.

You were enjoying your life and they came in to take everything you have. Be strong, be brave.

Bully sister put her down so much it took decades to come back up but when she did, best of luck.

BURPS, DIZZINESS AND BLOAT

Nausea, dizziness, bloat and burp. These all indicate the wrong diet for humans, this era's curse.

Burp. Hiccups. heartburn. Upper chest pain, bloating. NAUSEA. Avoid the carbs, end of trauma.

It was hard to believe the fruits weren't my answer for everything, that they even made me sickly.

The meat is the least likely allergen and there's no fiber. Eating just meat starts a new life flying clever.

It's hard to believe the meat wasn't the problem but the fruit was. It's all upside down I guess.

Being a meat-eater means being an intermittent faster cuz between meals you can go much longer.

FAST TO SEE/BE FREE

It's hard to believe my nausea, heartburn and burping was from fruit, it looked so innocent too.

I saw a little fruit as purifying the carnivore diet but all it did was add considerable discomfort.

Stopped all fruit and the nausea was GONE. Relieved, I swear off of those carbs forever, thank you God!

ALLERGIC TO EVERYTHING BUT MEAT

You're allergic to everything, concentric circles spreading out. Meat-only is left, heavenly route.

Start to fast, endure your nausea, eat meat when you can and look up as God takes over for man.

Do ulcers cause nausea and heartburn? Indeed they do but the carnivore diet stops all this soon.

Eat meat til fat's gone from the body. That includes cellulite & uglifications which are so unsightly.

Get thin sliced sirloin, fry both sides in butter--meal's done in two minutes, can it get any better?

How long's it take to cook pancakes? Not two minutes and you're left with the problems above ok.

Two minutes for beef meal then proceed with your adventurous creative day with a healthy feel.

Beef four times a week then bacon and eggs for three. That's seven meals a week--this is CHEAP!

LEFTIST DOINGS

1200 Jews slaughtered in their homes and the old hippies and kids are praising Hamas: cold.

206

FAST TO SEE/BE FREE

What if a group told us to cease fire after 911? We'd tell em to go to hell but this was even worse son.

Support Israel without conditions. Allow em to destroy Hamas or it's too late for western civilization.

COMPLETION

The closer I get to completion the more I feel carried along by a stream son: that's God alone.

Suddenly you realize everything is completing itself and you can't stop it. It's destiny, glorify in it.

When I wrote for the masses I couldn't separate myself fast enough then I blast off, no more cashless.

So today's Wednesday. See every day as a Saturday for an unplanned day of play, circuitous ok.

I'm almost WWII era, 1949. Now is an alien world I don't even wanna know, I'm a proud dinosaur, aye.

The more I approached the end of the project the more I felt pulled to the finish line as if by magic.

SOVEREIGNTY

WICKED BANDS
THE ONTOLOGICAL FATAL REALITY
THANK YOUR OPPRESSORS
SUFFERING BRINGS PERFECTING
LACK OF BOUNDARIES CAN KILL YOU
LONERS, SAINTS AND ECCENTRICS
YOUR VICTORY DAY: THE FAST
LIFE AND GUT CONSTIPATES
HOME LUXURIES AND COMFORTS
DEPTHLESS TERROR OF BETRAYAL
CRUTCH DEVELOPMENT
SEPARATE TRUE FROM FALSE
ANTISEMITISM RISING
THE LITMUS TEST OF CARNAGE
GO FORWARD NOW

SOVEREIGNTY

WICKED BANDS

So you married/you're now socially connected. Result: loss of self totally/not what you expected.

To be suddenly HOOKED to people is what is called "wicked bands". Control and sabotage man.

Suddenly two stepsons were living in my house. I entered hell on earth and a triple curse.

These connections are cobweb illusions of confusion and manipulation--so people seek libation.

Smooth the wheels, make it bearable. Stay mildly soused all day in another social reality that's all.

Husband starts drinking: his whole reality [about wife] changes while his social world rearranges.

It's the ontological fatal reality: your world is NOT what you thought it was/the bottom falls out.

THE ONTOLOGICAL FATAL REALITY

I felt the bottom of my gut drop off, my whole world upside down, betrayed and dumped.

She married smiling Jimmy but he turned out to be a haunted house taking her into insanity.

SOVEREIGNTY

It's the state of sin bringing denial so your world drops out without the social skills to resolve it.

When I got back at the foe little occurred. But when God vindicated me they died soon after.

You can find your destiny even in a busy city by building boundaries see, despite the great difficulty.

What are your talents and knacks? Work on those for success and leave the social to the hicks.

THANK YOUR OPPRESSORS

Thank God for oppressors for they taught us never to oppress another person forever, I swear.

Oppressors teach us all we need to know about how to be a leader: just to never be like they were.

Tho' it's horrible knowing him it made me very careful how I'm acting, seeing how I brought it on.

It's a system and a queen would not have evoked those reactions. Down deep you know that son.

Instead of letting a great book gather dust why not open it up anywhere and let synchronicity erupt?

I did it Lord. I ran the race/completed my work. I wanna do something else, I want home to come first.

I ran the race, I learned from my mistakes, I did things my way, I won at least in Your eyes I pray.

SUFFERING BRINGS PERFECTING

If you're unique enough to be a success you're gonna suffer the worst when down with the mass.

SOVEREIGNTY

It helps to know you had to go thru the burning. That's how you made gold, by boiling and hurting.

Since the formula says all recovery is elimination, fast on everything for financial freedom.

If a man due to need for approval can't stop gallivanting with other women that's why she leaves him.

She doesn't care what he looks like, he's reliable and pays the bills: what a woman needs.

They wanna be with you. If you need approval--everybody needs love--they'll destroy you.

They all wanted to be with me & I was taught to be a good hostess: no walls see. Decades of slavery.

My life had fullness but theirs was nothingness so they flowed in and I mal-adapted with mental illness.

LACK OF BOUNDARIES CAN KILL YOU

My lack of boundaries came close to being the end of me. I escaped to the desert to find destiny.

In the desert I flourished when alone but when people came I felt anguished, aggravated, let down.

After 3 decades on the Potter's Wheel finding self and destiny God replaced a cabin with a mansion.

I had only people problems my whole life. Now a high wall is etched in my DNA, I've had it, aye.

LONERS, SAINTS AND ECCENTRICS

Eccentrics--loners--live ten years longer than normals. Find a spouse who gives you space that's all.

SOVEREIGNTY

Take it from me, it's ok to be an eccentric loving being alone: cornucopia of creative insights, oh!

Fortunately I've a spouse who's the same way: two saints living in a house but separate/alone ok.

Without the protection of a like-thinking spouse, being alone is fraught with danger and seeking help.

Osteen: tho' terrified of public speaking when his dad died he had an urge/compulsion to speak see.

A few notes but other than that stay unplanned. Start here but then let the spirit take over man.

I rarely see him because we both love being alone but he pays the bills and protects the home.

She's socially connected, he isn't so marriage makes life easier that way—though now it's crowded.

YOUR VICTORY DAY: THE FAST

You can feel it: an appointed fasting day. This is the day of miracles, insights and revelations ok.

We get so used to eating we forget the bliss of fasting until life puts hurdles there for overcoming.

By doing nothing you're accomplishing everything. Nothing done yet nothing left undone see.

See this day's fast as an adventure: an inner journey of enlightenment to find self/God every minute.

Fasting is a selfix, a way of perfecting the engine and revealing ALL God has for us when done.

The fast: see EMPTINESS as the only way to exquisite FULLNESS of self, personality and destiny.

SOVEREIGNTY

LIFE AND GUT CONSTIPATES

Life and intestines constipate. The only way to break this jam is to fast [with God you have a date].

Today you break the log jam. It'll be FUN ma'am! A sudden psychic opening in the bright sun.

Add carbohydrates to the carnivore diet and you get nausea, heartburn, bloating, all of it!

Lucky me, I get a pound of bacon for breakfast, pepper steak for lunch then I fast for the hunch.

Remove fruit from the carnivore diet and you're rid of hiccupping, burping, nausea and bloating.

When you're competing with teenage porn stars you gotta keep up. That's plastic surgery in Utah.

The best way to do that is to live on animal fat. Cheese, butter, eggs if you can, just beef is best.

HOME LUXURIES AND COMFORTS

You get used to your own comfort/luxuries and forget what it's like to lose that sweet sovereignty.

A man appreciates female company but forgets what he's losing: his OWN ways, his very destiny.

A man's desire for sex influences what he selects and all else goes to hell it seemed to his ex.

I appreciate home comforts/luxuries and what I've selected, remembering when I had no effect.

They saw you as a hedonist when actually you were just totally traumatized [TT], you poor guys.

SOVEREIGNTY

Self-gentleness is the KEY. Everything else turns around after that as you recall the ugly.

Get into HOME. That means boundaries & not letting people in! They want IN, don't forget that friend.

It would be smooth sailing if all the wives and mothers didn't insist on all that produce eating.

"Inclusion" excludes Jews and Asians. That's one contradiction in these college administrations.

How can I be around your kids ma'am if they punish me or break my windows for correcting them?

DEPTHLESS TERROR OF BETRAYAL

The utter depthless terror when I suddenly saw the people I trusted go against me in anger.

To protect yourself against sudden implosion you must be prepared for people and all of their evil.

The minute I got married the world was nice to me. Before then it was brutal, a kind of tyranny.

I was even angry at the dead. I spent countless hours ruminating, resenting, remorsing, wasted.

God said don't fear evil, tho' it surrounds you constantly. They group up on the loner see.

It says in Psalms 1 that kings WOULD collude against God's man whom He would champion.

We are to expect wicked bands of collusion against us, especially in our home between bros/sis.

It was so hellish I sought seclusion all my life. People's hate for no apparent reason & scary strife.

SOVEREIGNTY

CRUTCH DEVELOPMENT

I had crutches to deal with the emotional pain of living amongst them, thus becoming a target of shame.

I don't see how you can stand being around them thinking that way. It's beneath you ok?

The see Israel as **WHITE** and **SUCCESSFUL** and thus it's ok for "oppressors" to be tortured that's all.

Because of this dyad in their head they can't sympathize with the oppressors even when dead.

SEPARATE TRUE FROM FALSE

Appreciating middle eastern music doesn't mean one is for Hamas. Learn to separate true from false.

Masked monsters with machine guns holding babies and old people in underground tunnels.

The delusion is we can change people by being nice. Not usually except in cases of love, aye.

There's no moral relativity here and the fact you think there is means you're sick and I'm done hick.

The people who hate Donald Trump continue to lie to us. He's the only way and they're scuzz.

The now palpable Jew hatred is rushing to the surface after the animalistic atrocity against em sis.

Their bloodthirsty attack was deliberately planned to incite Jew hatred everywhere in the land.

ANTISEMITISM RISING

Antisemitism: a Satanic spirit erupting with stress then it generalizes, like to anyone with darkness.

SOVEREIGNTY

It's all about oppressors-oppressed. They see Israel as white supremacists due to their great success.

The United Nations has a tremendous anti-Israel bias and you can see it in every committee sis.

Zionism means Jews having a place of safety, free of persecution. To not want that is Jew hatin'.

It's the LITMUS TEST: Can you condemn Oct 7 and Hamas? IF NOT, GOOD RIDDANCE!

Can't find Israel on a map and they don't know what apartheid means but they still hate all that.

Trump is a "dictator" because he wants a wall and he wants to drill, drill, drill? These are fools, all.

THE LITMUS TEST OF CARNAGE

I thought we were friends as we emailed all day for years. But Oct 7 split us for good: RUPTURES.

She avoided the carnage and only pitied the "freedom fighters". I was aghast--I thought I knew her!

The apathy of universities was the third shock as we now clearly SEE the problem since the 60's.

Reaction to Oct.7 was the litmus test dividing friends and family across the land. It's incredible man.

Free speech in the universities? Speak dissension from the party line and you're dead or pilloried.

"Harvard is dedicated to free speech". What a joke: say something different and you're banished.

To make things worse tyrants are arrogant, like Hitler youth as conservative speakers are banned.

SOVEREIGNTY

The sixtie's pothead hippies are grandparents to this new breed of brats and dictatorial Marxists.

Social psychology is a fascinating subject because we're dealing with **HERDS** with minds **FIXED**.

You can't change the herd's thought or direction easily--it takes time to re-adjust to a new beat see.

GO FORWARD NOW

Bible says we're to put childish things away and that includes memory if you wanna succeed ok.

One way to let bad past go [so you can go forward] is to return to youth/how you spent your hours.

LAST WORDS

YOU OVERCAME THE HERD
BRING IT UP TO LET IT GO
FEAR OF MOBS/COLLUSIONS
PEOPLE ARE MEAN
GOING BACKWARD IS HARD
THE STATE OF AMERICA
OBSTRUCTION #3: FOOD
RETURN TO FACTORY SETTINGS
CRAZY KITCHEN CONTRAPTIONS
HOW TO BOIL AN EGG
SHRIMP LOUIES & CHICKEN CAESARS
THE BEAUTIFYING FAT
FIND THE CULPRIT OF BLOATING
FIRST THE INTESTINES, THEN...
END GAME

LAST WORDS

As her authority grows so does h capacity for cruelty. The human element is positively scary.

Cuz I didn't listen to parents and elders I had to go thru hell to learn things on my own, for years.

Return to when you were a kid before the trouble started. Before you were warped by culture.

Return to childhood sovereignty before they broke you down from unique spirit to conformed clown

You had to go through hell cuz you didn't know enough to protect yourself. Stop complaining, build.

YOU OVERCAME THE HERD

As you fast take PRIDE you overcame the herd and the insanity in reaction to it: now go forward.

You've overcome the herd and the mental illness coming from maladapting to that curse.

They called you crazy but actually it was them systematically driving you there see.

Deep canyons are part of the Hero's Path and what comes from it is the Treasure Hard To Attain.

The primitive phase of the Savior Archetype is the madman or madwoman, just accept it man.

LAST WORDS

You had to go thru all that to get to here, perfection and happiness protected in your new sphere.

You had to go thru all that to get to here, perfection and protection in your new sphere.

BRING IT UP TO LET IT GO

Relive it all with the intention of letting it all go. You must or rust: jettison old baggage for success.

Don't go back into the past if you were one-down, frowned upon, spit on or treated sub human.

Don't put old scripts back into the computer. You gotta stay present where you're respected sister.

To go back DOWN is like an anchor on your spirit. Gotta stay high and old things, don't get near it.

You're filled with ego/hubris until you've had a stroke or something else beyond your control.

In the sin soaked season of treason, nothing goes right and everyone becomes a blight.

It was slippery. As soon as I found someone I could trust they'd always go in with the enemy.

Being the victim of herd tyranny/groupthink teaches us more than a library of books about the finks.

People hear something and fill their cup with it. They flip the script and that's it—you're. a twit.

FEAR OF MOBS/COLLUSIONS

I still shudder to think of Borrego tho' I've been gone ten years. Social psychology--MOBS--brings fear.

LAST WORDS

How easily the cruel collude together, planning how to take down God's man/woman forever.

The peeps COLLUDE: like peas in a pod, while you stay alone in your pursuits, blissfully unaware too.

It wasn't about demonstrating order but fear and power. Living with tyrants is cortisol stress every hour.

Dad was power wielded in the most malevolent form making him a recluse since leaving the farm.

Prepare for struggles if you won't conform to perverted male society's devices to break you down.

To be a queen you gotta hold your head up high. That's all my dad ever said, knowing the world, aye.

PEOPLE ARE MEAN

People are mean and they wanna bring you down--you upstart you--and the obstructions are cruel.

A famous professor ends in a concentration camp: just imagine the cruel put downs to level it up.

People are either apathetic or mean. The smilers are usually either virtual signalers or trained see.

Lack of education makes happy all the time. Learning about man makes us stern, divisive, fenced in.

Learning about what CAN happen makes us guarded, self-protective, careful, shrewd and quiet.

Learning how FAST life can change makes us careful, selective of words, contemplative, terse.

GOING BACKWARD IS HARD

LAST WORDS

After a period of independence, moving back to a bad home was a meat grinder for re-adaptants.

There IS no competition. You're in your OWN stream at your OWN steam pressure, that's all son.

After solving all his childhood problems he came into his own peculiar destiny with a new family.

THE STATE OF AMERICA

American cities are demolished and the baby boomers are homeless. Help us Lord, please bless.

Social psychology: how ambition & ideology intertwines to create figures of unspeakable cruelty.

The slaughter of Oct. 7 divided friends. All of a sudden the antisemitic spirit reared up: The End.

OBSTRUCTION #3: FOOD

Ok buddy I'm pulling out my main artillery. You've had it along with all my enemies, it's a fast see.

My kitchen was clogged with modern appurtenances. I have to laugh now when I think about it.

Your worst day can become your best day when you turn it around through a fast ok.

We went from pot roasts to Shrimp Louies and Chicken Caesars but so what it's still protein sir.

RETURN TO FACTORY SETTINGS

Fast to return to factory settings. Fast to overcome all things and fast just to be creative/happy.

It's hard to fast at first, I know. It's hard to get offa eating as a way to keep yourself stable/full.

LAST WORDS

It's a temporary measure, your trump card, a short vacation into cosmic land/seeing afar.

Do it. Prove yourself. Transcend hedonism or escapism. Fly above with angelic wisdom.

We may also define fasting as just eating less, and I also recommend just cheese in a fat-fast.

Kitchen gadgets: flip a switch and it comes out perfect. It doesn't! All I need is a pan & a pot, that's it.

Modern cookers that "come out perfect": well they don't mate. Stick to griddle or oven ok.

"Put it all together and turn it on". No, for the best cooking you tend, stir, braise, taste son.

CRAZY KITCHEN CONTRAPTIONS

I bought every kitchen contraption & gave em all away. A simple griddle & oven makes me so happy.

They're too complex when cooking should be joyous. Taste, add, tend, stir, braise, brown, sear!

Emerill makes it look so easy and tasty, doesn't he? What a scam it's all turned out to be, to me.

Older cooks go for pot roasts in the oven for hours, not chicken nuggets and fries in the air fryer.

What I have left: frying pans, oven pans and a countertop pizza maker for cheese man.

Boil eggs for the frig man and make doughless pizza with cheese, mushrooms, zuchini, onions.

No more slow cookers that take hours cuz they just don't taste good despite what ads put forth.

LAST WORDS

The pizza maker works great for omelettes put forget omelet makers, the texture/I just didn't like it.

The omelette maker may work great for cheese and veggies, try it. Add shrimp too, I like it.

Cheese is equal to meat in protein, I say make use of it. For snacks along with boiled eggs for sheen.

HOW TO BOIL AN EGG

Boil a buncha eggs, put in fridge. Bake a buncha bacon, that's your meal and have cheese later on.

Eggs: bring to boil, turn off heat and cover. To make them easy to peel, put in freezing water.

When you get hungry eat those eggs and enjoy your bacon, the best part of carnivore I reckon.

I also bake chicken breasts once a week and use them in chicken caesar salads or stir fries see.

After five months on carnivore my gut shrunk to a walnut, wow! It takes so little to feel full now.

For the BEST bacon: line up on pan, put in oven at 400 for 20 minutes, turn off to finish cooking.

For beef use thinly sliced sirloin for STIR FRY. Brown both sides, add soy sc/ginger/garlic mixture.

SHRIMP LOUIES & CHICKEN CAESARS

Make shrimp Louis salads or use it for stir fry. Either way this is a DELICIOUS trip I'd say, aye.

On the day I gave it all away we celebrated with a party and I fixed the most delicious cheese tray.

LAST WORDS

Beef tacos for keto: If still ketotic [no bloat] then have at it for there's nothing more delicious, no?

Bloat and breathing problems: there was no doubt I had an egg allergy and I never liked em.

Intestinal bloating from allergic inflammation: Eat something else, wait it out, learn your lesson.

How wonderful to return to slim normal after a period of bloating from a cycle of food sinning.

Stopped eating eggs and intestinal inflammation [BLOAT] dispersed, no more feeling worse.

THE BEAUTIFYING FAT

Ate greasy bacon, no problem just heaven. Ate a stick of butter, feel so moistened and enlivened.

Ate two sticks of butter, no problem whatsoever. Ate a pound of bacon and felt so good all over!

First it doesn't bother you/may even make you high, you can go for awhile then BAM: allergic reaction.

Ate a pound of bacon after swollen egg reaction and wow--I feel the body quickly slimming down.

Nothing more uncomfortable than a swollen abdomen and the way it looks too is godawful ma'am.

Swelling is YOUR body's reaction to what you ate. Some are so sensitive they swell easily ok.

I never liked eggs, they smell like sulphur/the sewer to me. Spiced or not, that was a sign of allergy.

FIND THE CULPRIT OF BLOATING

LAST WORDS

Once I found the culprit of bloating I never ate that again. That's how vanity can be your friend.

You eat some things and only LATER when it hits the colon will you react. Good info for the Elect.

You never see that [type of] person again and you never eat that food again: recovery is ELIMINATION.

It's AUTO-IMMUNITY. Your body's sensitive reaction to bad food and also bad people for you too.

Some times if you have a sudden autoimmune reaction to bad people you'll be called "hateful" too.

My body's reaction to bad food: bloat which I hate. My mind's reaction to bad people: shut the gate.

FIRST THE INTESTINES, THEN...

First the intestines bloat from inflammation, the lungs fill with mucus and then joints hurt man.

After years of fasting, frugal fruit then carnivore my gut shrunk to a walnut. So little is needed now.

So little mass is needed cuz I get my requirements from fat: collapsed mass/high nutrition in less.

But, like paleo man, I reversal dieted into fruit at times. Life is varied and then you re-adapt, aye.

Fruit or fauna [animal fat/meat] is the reversal and I'd draw the line there. No plants/processed fair.

END GAME

These are self-standing proverbs. You don't need context nor paragraph to dissolve the curse.

LAST WORDS

I do on average three perfect pages a day. At this point in my life it's written in my DNA as a writer ok.

I went crazy for part of my life. As I look back, it was nothing but bedlam with people in strife.

We're all gonna die now, our generation will be gone. Why not cut each other slack & get along?

Never call anyone from the past. why should you--have they called you? No, it's good riddance at last.

I long for the Great Work to be done. I wanna new life in the right brain, no need to write just have fun.

100,000 proverbs & 120 books, isn't that enough? I finished my work and it's homelife I love.

Weekend Fast: Party Blast

CAN'T REASON WITH EM
DON'T BLAME THE HORDES
THE WEEKEND FAST
FASTING IS OUR TRUMP CARD
FASTING TURNS THINGS AROUND
THE ANSWER TO STRIFE
ENTERING THE MAGIC LAND
CAN'T AFFORD NOT TO FAST
SWEET CAN MAKE YOU SWELL
OUR END TIMES
POST-COMPLETION
YOU COMPLETED YOUR ASSIGNMENT

Weekend Fast: Party Blast

Wife of Alcoholic Syndrome: He's Jolly Jimmy to the world while torturing wife behind closed doors.

As anosognosia lifts, you see your past clearly. It's kinda embarrassing but only temporary.

Those who call you sick are the sick ones. The good is always called evil in Satan's kingdom.

In the Wife of the Alcoholic Syndrome he cuts her down to size and she's blamed for it all besides.

Shut out the whole era--a past black out. It was your season of treason & you were someone else.

You gotta forget that guy, it's a soul tie. Release it cuz it's sexual and a demon blocking destiny.

Don't worry about your work, **COMPLETION** will attract pollination to the kernel, your creation.

Fear is **PAST** experiences appearing real. Nothing's happening now, it's all good but you **FEEL.**

CAN'T REASON WITH EM

If you can't reason with em, let em go. They'll only get more dangerous, like Hamas: more bold.

Seeing right requires depth of reasoning and they won't go deep: they stay on the party line see.

WEEKEND FAST: PARTY BLAST

Some generations are so deep in the brainwash, any dissidence can get you killed or bashed.

Most women are inferior thinkers: they are socially driven to reason and emotional worldviewers.

Many women are so emotionally driven they think nice can make a mass murderer more lovin'.

They end up getting innocents killed cuz they won't enforce discipline and order: NO WILL.

After grifting her $200 he came back later. She forgave him again, grateful for him as a suitor.

The world tore me down in my self esteem. Of course I brought it on with my crutches you see.

When hanging out with folk like that anything can happen and everything did so do past-blocking.

Stop paying off gossipers so they'll go easier on ya'. I did that for years but they still kill ya'.

DON'T BLAME THE HORDES

Don't blame the hordes streaming into your home, blame yourself for leaving the door open.

Illegal aliens: 20,000 a day to the U.S., 2000 a day to San Diego and 300 a day to El Cajon, Ca.

Reactions to Oct. 7 showed us we must re-evaluate all our alliances: who are our friends/who isn't.

Their master vision is One-Worlders. That means America has no sovereignty: Open Borders.

THE WEEKEND FAST

WEEKEND FAST: PARTY BLAST

The fast is the device that God hath chosen for man. But animals also do it naturally and often.

Fasting evens things up: it's a military device. You don't wine and dine to man up, you SACRIFICE.

What we ended up with here: pizza, popcorn, salads, stiry fry, tacos, bacon, eggs and butter.

You want mouse meals of high potency [HQ] foods. With me it takes so little it's really cool.

Over-fullness is a severe encumbrance. If I overeat I wished I hadn't and quickly learn to curb it sis.

Then there's the weekend fast, Fri pm-Mon am, for 60 hours. A deep rest then God will shower.

As long as I'm fasting I'm the queen, the king, the exemplar, the prince or princess see.

As long as I'm fasting I'm the queen, the king or anything else I jolly well done wanna be.

See the fast as a special party--a blast--to do it justice. See opportunity not just weight loss.

The fast is God's divine device to get solutions, more power or manifestation of your ideas.

Even if temporary the mere decision to fast will make it easier next time entering the gold mine.

FASTING IS OUR TRUMP CARD

Fasting is our trump card when all else fails. Things WILL RESOLVE, keep this thought central.

In your weekend fast you will drop all excess water and intestinal debris. It's. a refreshing breeze.

WEEKEND FAST: PARTY BLAST

Fast til' Monday--can you do that with me? We'll have a ball this weekend, like another world see.

When fasting you're laying the ground for a million dollar hunch. You're turning things to high as such.

Instead of memory embarrassment, look at all you've overcome. Let the fast recall it in sum.

Let your fasting weekend be something you'll never forget, and return to it often for your selfix.

FASTING TURNS THINGS AROUND

Fasting turned things around a million times. I always saw it as a way to overcome Goliath, aye.

Fasting overcomes eaters. They're down in the gut always digesting while you're rare achievers.

That feeling of being a stranger in a strange land will pass as the fast enlarges consciousness.

Gotta stop writing to enjoy my fasting day. But the more I fast the more God tells me to say.

Weekend fast, party blast. Let that be your slogan for the next sixty hours as all misery is passed.

Get into the moment, turn the music up. Turn the music off, listen to the wind or rain on the rooftop.

THE ANSWER TO STRIFE

It's the answer to strife, God's military device: sacrifice. Building a strong will so no food can entice.

With IBS/digestive issues you're burping all thru the day anyway, so why not take a break today?

WEEKEND FAST: PARTY BLAST

Every time you denounce an urge the will becomes stronger. Soon you're a champion faster/winner.

Another suggestion is the fat-fast: eat a piece of cheese when hungry then get right back.

You can try a fat-fast with fatty macadamia nuts but I think it's gotta be FAUNA: only animal fats.

Fast as long as you can and break with doughless pizza for your one meal a day, also known as OMAD.

For INFO on fat-fasting and lacto-fruitarianism [cheese] read the five KK books from 2001.

ENTERING THE MAGIC LAND

You're hungry. Should you break it with pancakes or enter the magic land? Persevere man.

The fast is nothing strenuous, it's a time of great rest. Lay down often if you need to: think/RELAX.

The fast is a time of weight loss—who doesn't want that? I feel so much better after ditching fat.

Enduring hunger pain is a show of how much you love God. That's how i handle it and turn it off.

With intestinal blockage we all feel like garbage. The fast is like a Drano add unblocking sludge.

Substitute DREAMING for hunger. Think of the sacrifice looking forward to the reward in the future.

Fast until the problem is resolved. That includes whether or not you've changed your goals.

As saints have shown, there are great rewards to austerity: fasting, celibacy, modesty, living lowly.

WEEKEND FAST: PARTY BLAST

Fast until you're stomach and abdomen is flat. A big belly: really, you gotta get rid of all that.

CAN'T AFFORD NOT TO FAST

You can't afford not to fast. There's not only too much to lose but you'll miss the gold ring again Mack.

It would be good to then fast every weekend, eating five meals a week. The superior diet is most cheap.

Substitute a desire for otherworldly visions over a satisfied gut. Get beyond the carnal rut.

Eating is the biggest crutch in this world and fasting is the greatest solution to all we abhor.

Don't eat and block that guy out for just one weekend. This is a turning point in your life friend.

Fasting brings on ENANTIODROMIA: a reversal or flip-flop where the bottom becomes the top.

This could be all you need to do: that ONE little change that brings on a TOTAL LIFE REVOLUTION.

Went on animal protein for the skin, went back to figs and the whole system switched back again.

You'll look ageless in the one system but you'll look your age in the other one--that's the problem.

SWEET CAN MAKE YOU SWELL

Fruit is too much fiber/water without giving the satiety and power I want: need FAUNA/animal fat.

Fig fast: was uncomfortably full all day with visible skin erosion from the lack of protein: hmmmm.

WEEKEND FAST: PARTY BLAST

I can eat so little it must be HQ: high protein, high fat animal food, coming in least mass too.

Over-fullness is devastation to energy. We don't want it ever again so stick to what you know see.

When you DO eat, it's gotta be HQ for satiety to make it to the next day as a daily fastarian ok.

Not 30 bananas in your one meal but one lamb chop bringing satisfied balance all through.

We can't take it anymore: massive meals. We want low mass/high nutrition and that means animal.

A piece of cheese for breakfast and I'm full all day. It's so efficient—I'll say it's heaven living this way.

One hard boiled egg fills me up all day. What efficiency—it's the HQ foods that pave the way.

OUR END TIMES

Terse verse and timed rhymes: whoda thought I'd end up advancing a theory using this device?

To fully appreciate ELDERING, let the past go. Those PTSD memories can kill you ya' know.

Relocation: I was so happy to leave California. People are so nice here, they leave ya alone, yah.

I completely forgive you but don't want you in my life. Sorry but why should I it was only strife.

Stay away from me trouble. I doubt you could ever find me now and besides we have a wall.

Popularity does not determine truth. Remember that or be swept up by mere numbers in a feud.

WEEKEND FAST: PARTY BLAST

Instead of being stuck in repeated memory, let your eyes go out to eternity/your own rarity.

POST-COMPLETION

Nowadays you gotta get an agent to get an agent. It's way too daunting so I'll let God handle it.

What are you supposed to do if you're a recluse? Get an agent to get an agent & wait for God too.

You've done it, the work is DONE. This will attract pollination so send it out and all doors open.

You gotta live right, ok? Cuz they can come and get you any day: things turn fast/can get creepy.

Before God rewards you He's gotta know you're gonna live right [this time]. NOW He showers, aye.

YOU COMPLETED YOUR ASSIGNMENT

You did it, you completed your assignment. You endured hunger and living in the basement.

You endured isolation and being misjudged by everyone. You learned to love being alone.

While they were out socializing/wasting their time you were devotedly doing your work inside.

The main thing is: you started the ball rolling. Now just let it go to the end with you in the receiving.

The main thing: it's a DESTINY and you came into perfection gradually, patiently, consistently.

The main point was you repented of that sin. We all know where we've been and God is watchin'.

WEEKEND FAST: PARTY BLAST

Free at last, all your talents are blessed and it's a blast as all archetypes are released for success.

A good writer is a pure vessel. It's a daily routine with you keeping clear of bad influences too.

Just do your work, complete it. Now start the ball rolling and stay high till the cycle's ended.

To hear an old man using language like that--forget him! If men can't grow up you're better off without him.

CRUSHED SPIRITS

DRESS RIGHT AND SPEAK TRUTH
RAISED BY ANOTHER WOMAN
I WASN'T READY FOR THAT
LOVE AND REALITY BETRAYED
CLEAR THE DECKS TO FIND SELF
EVERYTHING CHANGES ALONE
ENSCONCED IN HIX POLITIX
THE DEVIL TAKES OVER
ANOSOGNOSIC BLINDNESS
HUMAN INVASION IS SUBTLE
FEMALES ARE INVADED
HYPER-CARNIVORE
FRUIT FIRST THEN FAT [FAUNA]
TO THE STUDENTS
SAGACIOUS ELDERING

CRUSHED SPIRITS

The sagacious stage of ELDERING is absolutely thrilling. Mining the past for gems and reliving.

All in one day this revolution occurs where the spirit's crushed and love is destroyed for years.

There were three stepkids. The third was a whoremonger so I had that to deal with in spirit.

They myth of "loving togetherness" is nothing but horribleness. Dear Lord I'll never forget it.

They're so adapted to crowds they don't even notice them now. That's our main difference God.

A woman with a Jezebel spirit will deride you to her friends, even set one up as her hit man.

They tried to hold me back, they stripped me of my cash. But I overcame if all cuza God my Dad.

We all have a bad past. Don't remorse for the path to victory's filled with canyons teaching us best.

When you work for the devil it's hell to pay. They're high on the hog one day then they're dead ok.

As a soul tie diminishes, out comes your intelligence. Like a breath of fresh air/you'll be lovin' it.

It's the light of a new day as all charisma vaporizes for that guy you see, delusion works that way.

CRUSHED SPIRITS

DRESS RIGHT AND SPEAK TRUTH

Women: just dress modestly, speak the absolute truth and then don't fear the [silly] enemy.

If it's truly a discovery let it be discovered. Don't you promote it cuz it's too big and you know it.

It's the virtue signalers who cause the most dam trouble cuz what they do is wrong then it doubles.

Don't ever come under their authority and that includes getting in their car. This is being smart.

Don't EVER come under their authority and that includes letting them in: not your friends!

You gotta mind your back constantly, ready for all possibilities. It's a human jungle see.

People are cruel and women are the cruelest to each other, even between mother & daughter.

Mother in law problems or stepmother syndrome is all part of a crazy situation in modern homes.

Broken families welded together, like a teen stepson saying he despises you like none other.

Or a thirty year old stepdaughter who hates your guts being in competition with you for her father.

They degraded her and she didn't even know it. That is the pitiful anosognosia of the love addict.

RAISED BY ANOTHER WOMAN

They were raised by another woman with different values--and boundaries--than you man.

CRUSHED SPIRITS

I instantly felt wickedly **TRAPPED** by my shrewdly sadistic teenage stepson. What a weddin'.

"He was so wicked & diabolical I didn't know how to handle it & got drunk-- and that was it." Lady

These interlocking jealousy triangles are like Greek tragedies which always occur in families.

You're caught in a mental trap of which you're unaware unless you're savvy about this stuff here.

It was the beginning of the end--the wedding--meeting his teen son and hateful mother, amen.

I WASN'T READY FOR THAT

I wasn't ready for that! It was heaven just him and I but add this other system and I wanted to die.

Unless you're studying this stuff it's like you're caught in a vice as your self-esteem is crushed.

I wasn't ready for that as an eccentric recluse and they being seasoned social manipulators too.

I can still remember gut aches in this matrix. I didn't know what the hell's happening/just felt sick.

It's social psychology man, they're screwing with your head. It's all about who's superior Fred.

Women are by far the worst. For description read Ceremony of the Innocent by Taylor Caldwell first.

LOVE AND REALITY BETRAYED

Here we were in love, then his mom and son come for the weddin'. I take the plunge then ended it.

CRUSHED SPIRITS

If the most beautiful women are men knowing how to put makeup on, why not you too woman?

Due to loss of identity/being betrayed it took me 30 years on the Potter's wheel to find myself ok.

I became an empty vessel, gutted and with gut ache. I had to find myself in the things I like/dislike.

What did I like? Studying all day, keeping people away and writing all night in my own world ok.

These boundaries/knacks were me. Achievements were me too--that's how you build identity.

CLEAR THE DECKS TO FIND SELF

You gotta be alone to find these markers of "you". Otherwise you're always adapting to people.

You can live in the quaintest town on earth but if it's filled with crowds what's it really worth?

I want just me and God not millions of distractions all around. It's a madhouse, leave me alone!

Grew up in La Mesa. It's the quaintest town--high end now. Filled with crowds/how can I love ya.

I have three acres for just me and mine. I never see anyone and it's a very rare situation, aye.

EVERYTHING CHANGES ALONE

When it's just you and the universe you've a whole other set of priorities, let us say the "most & first".

To re-enter society after an era of solitude in nature is so strange I swear. Another reality/false layer.

CRUSHED SPIRITS

It's an artificial reality made up of events, places, petty competitions and dramas in America.

I did it: I overcame society's pull and conquered loneliness and anxiety over things futile.

In La Mesa you're constantly going to new restaurants and shops: an outer reality non-stop.

Disneyland: A totally outer reality of distractions. It's what kids want or people who are avoidin'.

What good is Europe if there's no place to park. Seek solitude in nature, you'll see it's the lark.

Eccentrics avoid crowds you see: after solitude you're past the point of wanting to be seen.

Eccentrics march to their own drummer and crowds are like static in a radio to a reclusive insider.

In a plastic social reality all seem nice 'til you go down a rabbit hole with any one of em/are enticed.

ENSCONCED IN HIX POLITIX

Wars, rumors of wars and open borders. Could there be any better indication that it's all over?

Our shrewd adversaries see Biden's pattern of risk avoidance and it's bringing hell in on us.

We've come to the point of choosing our battles. Don't waste energy on futile debates for example.

Liberals are lawless and always take advantage when in power with FLOODS of invaders every hour.

Political scientists look at PERCEPTIONS since true or false, that creates dangerous revolutions.

CRUSHED SPIRITS

Once a falsehood gathers mass velocity it doesn't matter true or false, just fence up quickly.

THE DEVIL TAKES OVER

Once they get a leg up they come & kill all the whites who are forever seen as oppressors, yikes.

Just like in South Africa, whoever is doing better is seen as an evil oppressor and for them it's over.

Those for open borders eat their words when a 1000 shopping centers are massacred in one day sirs.

What can we do? What can any cog in the wheel do other than live that day/stay cheerful too?

You know how they think and how far they will sink so be stoically gracious and endure the finks.

We're talking about liberals who condone baby killing and Oct. 7. They are callous, don't you see it?

If they think and CONDONE those things have nothing to do with finks—with aristocratic reserve see.

Reserve: You've gotten too chummy with the enemy, an appeasement posture like timid puppies.

They don't think like you do. We're talking VALUES. That's what matters not their skin color too.

How do they treat dogs? That's your barometer of how things matter—herds are different brother.

If you were a slave would you rather have a white or black master? Study the matter then answer.

Instead of busy freeways I want dirt roads and cowboy fences then three acres of just-me-ness.

CRUSHED SPIRITS

It's a terrible illness that affects queens. Women in history: you gotta look at it that way see.

ANOSOGNOSIC BLINDNESS

Healed from addiction & whole again, anosognosia begins to disperse and you begin seein'.

At the time she was filled with evident blind spots like a whole part of personality was blocked out.

It saved her from undue strain when forging ahead despite the crutches keeping her sane.

It was pop-pop-pop as memories alit. An events from 20, 30, 5 years ago were unveiled I had a fit.

You don't see the system at the time. That's the devil in addiction, keeping you blindly sick, aye.

HUMAN INVASION IS SUBTLE

I'm retired, relocated and live freely within walls and lovely gates. But yet I still feel invaded ok.

People are grabby, mean & controlling if you let em in but before that they're nice aren't they friend?

You gotta spot the change. Compare their delivery to their promises and then quickly disengage.

I was afraid of stepson and mother in law: bottomless pits, deep caverns and wolves, oh God.

The wedding was the ending. After the family shock there was no reconciling & it began imploding.

The wicked bands of other people: they are so controlling, presumptuous, assuming, evil.

FEMALES ARE INVADED

CRUSHED SPIRITS

If female they feel entitled to a piece of you and here's where strength comes in: boundaries man.

Most lower females have a Jezebel spirit and these make lousy girl friends. Boundaries man.

Jezebels will either take over your life when given the chance or RUIN it with gossip of the past.

Don't take anyone's advice. For who are they to advise you? Unless you asked, fly above/stay high.

Bring impoverished people into a nation of wealth and that country will collapse into socialist hell.

First your fig fast then your fat fast. That's called hyper-carnivore, reversal dieting, having a blast.

No matter how beautiful a place is the crowds wreck it for me. We all should examine our reality.

You can spend a lot of money on useless things you know. Don't change if happy with home.

HYPER-CARNIVORE

Anything with a seed is a fruit. A diet of fruit and meat fulfills all requirements and is delicious too.

I felt magical in this food reversal. Figs in the morning then switching to eggs/meat/fat-fasting.

In hypercarnivore we may eat high carb fruits but no veggies, starches or any processed foods.

Low carb fruits are often seen as veggies: bell peppers, eggplants, tomatoes, olives, squash.

When I added fruit I came alive. I didn't feel that well all meat/eggs but with both I felt great/thrived.

CRUSHED SPIRITS

My weight came down too. Using high-carb fruits for the first meal did not put on pounds, whew!

FRUIT FIRST THEN FAT [FAUNA]

If you're a daily fastarian you can expect miracles every day man: "magic coincidences" said Jung.

You're above the human race down in the gut digesting all the time while you've transcended time.

Boil eggs, put em in the frig. Eat figs for the morning meal then for the day eat those eggs.

When hunger strikes you're ready to eat PROTEIN, PROTEIN, PROTEIN! Or the figs to CLEAN.

I know I need protein, that's the second meal. Boiled eggs for snacks or stir fry is delicious/unreal!

Then you fast: JUST SKIP DINNER. Give yourself an 18 hour complete rest so energy rises upward.

I've been doing this since age 16 when my grades went from D to A by the mere switch of routine.

Dried figs keep forever at my desk, giving six more hours of work uninterrupted by breakfast.

My work time is extended by the second meal. boiled eggs at my desk then the nooner, a meat fest.

This plan along with daily fasting will mean every day and minute is perfect & you can take action.

With an unplanned food life my days were erratic and unpredictable. Heartburn, all kinds of trouble.

With fruit and meat, it's smooth sailing. Fruit first then the animal fat [fauna] then afternoon fasting.

CRUSHED SPIRITS

The figs are for cleansing and maximum regularity. Then the protein builds strength and beauty.

DON'T FEAR BACON GREASE

Stop fearing bacon grease and butter when you should be fearing fakes like margarine and others.

Use bacon grease for your skin before you'd put all those extremely expensive chemicals on it.

Fear what you should be fearing--anything man is creating--but not God's created things.

I am happiest/strongest eating breakfast only. As a Scotswoman it's a tradition in my family.

Breakfast is when we're altogether, for who knows where we'll end up? It puts us on top.

Boil eggs for the frig, put pound of bacon in oven. Eat the protein/fat meal, now you're done.

No more eating for entertainment, it takes too much time. No more eating for others, it's a lie.

You wanna be skinny for longevity. How could I get fat with dried figs, a few eggs and bacon see?

And yet I'm fully satisfied all day, it's called SATIETY. SP--Satiety Power--are the best foods see.

What did those skinny beauties of the fifties eat? Cottage cheese, boiled eggs and also meat.

It's uncanny how food with low mass [e.g. bacon] brings satiety--all day it lasts. But that's how it works.

They say I'm too restrictive, choosing only the best. But people got well in the depression/on much less.

CRUSHED SPIRITS

FORGET HUGE SALADS

As a vegan I ate huge bowls of salads to feel full. Even with avocados I was never satisfied though.

With bacon and eggs it doesn't matter if you skip the second meat meal, it's enough for real.

I prefer fruit at night to wake up cute and purified. Dried mission figs are so practical, what a find.

Fruit-only made me skinny fat but fruit and meat made me slender but muscular without cellulite.

I love having the food BEHIND me, so the whole day I'm working creatively not thinking of food see.

What did the old cowboys get in town? Coffee & bacon but also sugar and flour if with a woman.

Once skinny some go back to rice, potatoes and bread but I wouldn't chance it, stay sharp instead.

Well that about does it, gonna get on with my day. I'm so excited every day, it's great living this way.

Things change: when you go back it's never the same. Don't look back for God's always here ok.

TO THE STUDENTS

Like C.R. Johnson said, let every day be a Saturday. An unplanned day of play always creatively.

I'm done with my work and the latest book: After The Great Work. I'm going to speak for sure.

No more Monday-Tuesday-Wednesday crap. From now on it's all the amazing same if you're on top.

CRUSHED SPIRITS

You pray for success and God gives His best: seeing your Self and all of its evident gifts.

When you see your Self and all it's evident gifts you just relax into God's well-timed, perfect plans.

No nose pressed up against the glass wanting in! Pull back into your own groove, all else is sin.

It never matters how great something is if there's crowds around it--can you not see this?

It's suffocating being a stranger in a strange land but it's especially brutal if it's one's own family.

Accept it and go on. Life's too short to worry about not fitting in, your destiny is too high/glistenin'.

SAGACIOUS ELDERING

God said "just open your mouth and I'll put in the words". From here on faith comes first.

The complacent city mob is happy as a lark while you're scared to death cuz you know best.

You see potential danger & heartbreak everywhere cuza of all your studies and experience [rare].

Due to your deep empathy/sagacity it's just easier to live apart and attract students and cohorts.

Can the sagacious live among the complacent? Well enough but only if not real expressive.

They don't like hearing anything which is true if it's negative. Everything must be pseudo-positive.

A shrewd devil sits on your shoulder bringing up the past to embarrass or piss you off forever.

CRUSHED SPIRITS

With every adrenalin rush in response to a triggering memory the devil wins over you squarely.

Suddenly it's all too much, gotta clear the decks. Then suddenly you get a hunch/remove the hex.

You're in total safety and comfort but your mind is stuck in the past when devalued and trod under.

This is where gratitude comes in. By taking stock of good things, PTSD memories begin to dim.

You're NOT in a tiny cabin victimized by invaders but in a mansion with a wall so it's just you there.

Let the past go, you weren't protected sis due to complacent, distracted ignorance I guess.

You were sick, fogged, ignorant or drugged. Forget it now, life's too short and you've a big job.

I've been there: did something profoundly stupid or selfish then pestered by constant remorse.

That's the Good News of Jesus Christ: He erases the past and puts you back on top, a promise.

Man may not forget it but God buries sin in the bottom of the ocean with a sign "don't go fishin'".

Take the day off, enjoy the weekend, clear the decks son. From clutter to clarity: victory won.

It's a two speed week. Work then relax. ENJOY the weekend break: the right brain/being lax.

Get used to two speeds. You WORK, you're off and RELAX. Learn to get off and stay off/no texts.

100 KAREN KELLOCK BOOKS

THE HERD IN WORDS
HIX POLITIX
HOW THEY RUINED US
JUST SKIP DINNER
LE FEMME AND THE COMMUNIST SPIRIT
LIBERAL CHAOS & ROT
LIBERAL DOUBLETHINK
LIBERAL GALL 1 & 2
LIBERAL SHOVE-DOWNS
LOCK YOUR GATE
LOSERS and Femme Fatales
MANUAL FOR SUPERIOR MEN
MODERN ART FROM HELL
MOSTLY FAKE
NOTES TO CHAMPS 1 & 2
OVERCOME FRENEMIES
PC MAKES US CRAZY
PEOPLE ARE CRUEL
PEOPLE PROBLEMS 1 & 2
PERSECUTED GENIUIS
POLI-PSYCH MYSTERIES
PRETENTIOUS SLOBS
QUEEN BEE
RED NEW DEAL
RETURNING TO FIRST NATURE
SEASON OF TREASON
SEPARATE MEANS HOLY
SOCIAL HYPNOTISM
SOLITUDE SOLUTION
SUPERCILIOUS
THE SCHOOLS SCREWED EM UP
TOAD TO PRINCE
TRIALS CYCLES
TRUMP VS. GROUP
TRUST IN TRASH
THE TRUTH ABOUT PEOPLE
UNDERHEANDEDLY CLEVER
WALK TALL WITHIN WALLS
WE'RE NOT ALL ONE
WINNERS SKIP DINNER
WORK OR SMERK

KAREN KELLOCK PH.D.

M.S. Political Science, San Diego State. Ph.D. in Psychology, University of California Irvine. Postdoctoral: UCI School of Medicine, Dept. of Psychiatry [NIMH Grants]. Developed the Debris Theory of Disease, a theory of system pathology in 120 books and 22 textbooks for the general public. The theory has a general formula: All disease is obstruction, all recovery is elimination, all success is attraction. The three obstructions are people, habit and food. Remove obstruction and snap to your goals, waiting in the wings.

Made in the USA
Las Vegas, NV
06 January 2024

83709987R00144